Six Plays
in
American History

Six Plays in American History

WRITTEN BY

HENRY H. WALSH

Illustrations by Robert MacLean

THE STEPHEN GREENE PRESS

BRATTLEBORO, VERMONT · 1969

PS
3573
A4755

Contents

166209

ABOUT THE AUTHOR,
HENRY WALSH, AND THIS BOOK

Henry Walsh's achievements are a direct refutation of the canard that maintains "those who can, do; those who cannot, teach." Beginning in 1934 as a teacher—of art, education, social studies, history, and playwriting—his career branched out into professional script writing with NBC and CBS for the popular *Thin Man* and *Inner Sanctum* radio series and for the prize-winning *You Are There, American Heritage, Cavalcade of America,* and *The Columbia School of the Air.* (For the latter, he also collaborated on the preparation of the Teachers' Manuals and ot'.er supplementary materials.) He has acted as network program planner as well as radio and TV playwright.

Other highlights of the Henry Walsh career are: an inservice training program for the New York City Board of Education in Activity Programming for Elementary Schools, during which time he founded and directed The Workshop, a teacher training program in art and handcrafts; an experimental workshop course in educational radio and TV and playwriting for children's theater at Sarah Lawrence College; service for the Puerto Rican Insular Government formulating and developing radio programming for education, and as writer and publication consultant for the Ittleson Center for Child Research. He is at present American History teacher at the Antioch-Putney Graduate School for Teacher Education. He has worked from time to time with school groups, both elementary and high school, in producing plays, his own and others.

We asked Mr. Walsh to provide for each play in this collection an introductory fill-in on the historical background of the action and practical suggestions for staging, properties, and casting for school production. Because of wide variation in school courses and methods, we have not included supplemental reading lists. Again, acting on Mr. Walsh's own experience with varying individual school and classroom approaches, we have omitted age/grade classifications as being either restrictive or misleading. For example, one of the plays has (in manuscript) already attracted educators interested in producing it at *both* the elementary and college levels. THE EDITOR

Foreword

I choose to believe that there is no *past* history, for, from one age to another, from one people to another, the story of mankind is continuous and ever flowing, expressing the total effects of individuals striving together to satisfy their material and spiritual needs. I believe, too, that all the turbulent emotional ingredients in human social development are the same basic elements that make for effective stage drama which can add flesh, bone and blood to history as a subject for study.

The first duty of a playwright is to hold his audience from opening line to final curtain; therefore, in writing an historical play, the records of history are his tools, not his masters. Nevertheless, even though he is functioning as a dramatist and not strictly as an historian, he should be called to account if blind bias, superficial research, or disregard for the cause and effect of historical progression has allowed him to present distortions of truth or falsifications of situation and character.

As I wrote the plays in this volume I felt a further responsibility, because I wanted them to be presented by and for students of American history. Therefore I imposed upon myself continuously two additional restraints, which take the form of questions.

One deals with dramatic pacing—telescoping or altering the time sequence of minor incidents that occurred within the major historical event in order to achieve greater effectiveness on the stage—and it is this: Would the final or climactic moment in this segment of history have been altered in any measurable degree by such a change? This of course poses the problem of causality, and the writer must do as much soul-searching as researching to resolve it.

Through the second question I screened the details used to create three-dimensional characterization: Would the real person in history, judging from all available source material involving his activity, have behaved in the manner in which I have presented him? This is a simpler matter to answer than the first one, because characters are much easier than events to judge in retrospect.

The six plays vary in level of theatrical sophistication, as they do also in level of content. However, all were designed to be playable in junior and senior high schools—and designed with the hope that they will stimulate a lively interest in the dynamic and fascinating story of America.   H. H. W.

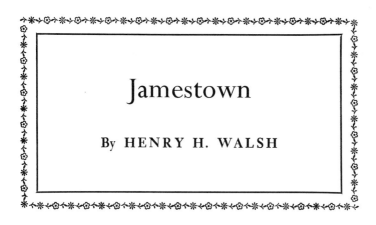

Jamestown

By HENRY H. WALSH

JAMESTOWN

CHARACTERS: 6 males

PLAYING TIME: 20 minutes

SET: One

✍️ Historical Notes

ON AN APRIL MORNING in the year 1607, three ships
under the command of Christopher Newport dropped
anchor in Chesapeake Bay off the shore of Virginia. The
vessels contained 150 men sent by the London Company to establish the first permanent settlement in the
New World. Among the passengers were George Percy,
the handsome younger son of the Earl of Northumberland;
the Reverend Robert Hunt, a Church of England clergyman; and Captain John Smith, adventurer. These three,
among others, have given us firsthand accounts of the
founding and early experiences in Jamestown.

Percy's *Observations* offers a vivid report of their landing
and preliminary explorations to find a suitable site for the
settlement. He starts with an enthusiastic description of the
land, a veritable Garden of Eden, described poetically, in a
manner indicating an extremely sensitive nature. But later
a note of sad disillusionment permeates his report. He talks
of famine, Indian attacks, and diseases. Percy never saw England again, and died of malaria in 1608.

Robert Hunt, one of the few selfless and devoted characters
in the settlement, came not to seek riches but to serve his
God and the greedy, rapacious adventurers who comprised
the bulk of the settlers. It was from one of his letters to his
bishop in London, rejecting the offer of the parish of Almondsbury and announcing his decision to remain in "James
City," that the theme of the play was suggested. He writes:
"May I first thank your lordship for reserving me the parish
of Almondsbury after I had advised you of my intent to

3

return to England. I beg your lordship's forgiveness for the concern you may have exercised in my behalf, but I have decided to remain in James City. When I account to you the reason for my decision, your lordship will agree that it was God's will that I do so. . . ." Robert Hunt never returned to England. He, too, died of malaria, in the year 1608, shortly after dispatching his letter.

Hunt's and Percy's accounts are quite at odds with the fanciful narratives of Captain John Smith: *A True Relation of such occurrences and accidents of noate as hath happened in Virginia since* . . . etc. etc. And in another book: *The True Travels, Adventures and Observations of Captaine John Smith,* published in 1630, Captain Smith presents a most entertaining tale, reminding one of the adventures of Baron Munchausen—only Smith meant to pass it off as factual. It was from this later narrative that we first heard the story of Pocahontas and how she saved the Captain's neck: a very dubious tale, which may have happened to John Rolfe (if it ever happened at all), the one who did marry the Indian "princess," the daughter of Powhatan. It was this same John Rolfe who discovered "gold" in the cultivation of tobacco, and saw it become one of Virginia's leading exports to England by 1619, despite King James the First's ban on tobacco in 1620: ". . . to sowe set or plant or cause to be sowen set or planted . . . formerly sowen or planted, but should forthwith utterly destroy and root up the same . . . as endangering and imparing of the health of our Subjects . . ." And 1619 was also the year that the first Negro slaves were brought to the continent and sold in Jamestown, thereby sowing the seeds of America's greatest shame and trial, unresolved even to this day.

✍ Production Notes

❪ Characters

THE REVEREND ROBERT HUNT, a Church of England clergy-
man
GEORGE PERCY, a younger son of the Earl of Northumber-
land
EDWARD BROWN, a commoner, product of London slums
FIRST SOLDIER, a stolid, professional adventurer
CAPTAIN JOHN SMITH, military leader of the Colony in
Jamestown
SECOND SOLDIER

❪ Scene

The interior of a church in the Colony of Jamestown just
after dawn, in the year 1608.

❪ Setting

A section in the interior of a roughly-built church of thatch
and split log. To the left is the altar, which is in sharp
contrast with the primitive surroundings, for it has been
carried from England to the colony. An altar cloth covers
the entire table. On the altar top are two candlesticks and
a Bible. The back panel consists of a triptych—a threefold
screen—decorated with separate pictures of related religious subjects. The altar rests on a raised dais. Several
backless benches face the altar. Light enters from two high
windows set in the back wall. A wide church door, barred
and barricaded with some benches, is right center.

❪ Costumes

The soldiers are in the uniform of the English military of
the early 17th century: metal helmet, breastplate worn

5

over a wide-sleeved doublet, pantaloons tucked into soft leather boots. Hunt is wearing Church of England vestments: a loose black gown and bands around his throat—a clergyman's collar of the Anglican Church. George Percy is dressed as an English aristocrat, but the cloth is torn and shabby. He has a sword at his side. Brown's clothing is hardly more than filthy rags. Captain John Smith is in the dress of a soldier, but sports a ruff around his throat and a colorful ostrich plume in his helmet, distinguishing his superior military rank. He also wears a sword.

❨ Properties

A church altar, altar-cloth and candlesticks, Bible, a straw pallet, a blanket, several backless benches.

❨ Lighting

The effect of feeble dawn light.

"Jamestown"

Jamestown

SCENE

The interior of a roughly built church of thatch and split log. The altar, left center, rests on a raised dais, which is in sharp contrast with the crudity of the building, for it has been carried from England to the colony. A few rows of backless benches face the altar. Feeble daylight enters from two shoulder-high windows on the back wall. A wide church door, barred and barricaded with some benches, is at right center.

At curtain rise HUNT, PERCY, BROWN and the FIRST SOLDIER are on stage. PERCY is sprawled on a bench, with one boot removed and a pantaloon leg split up the side and folded back to expose a wound which HUNT is bandaging with strips of cloth torn from a kerchief. An arrow lies on the floor near PERCY's foot. The SOLDIER is standing at the window, musket in hand, peering out cautiously. BROWN is lying on a straw pallet with his back resting on the wall to the right of the altar. His legs are covered with a ragged blanket. He looks ill, appears to be somewhat delirious with fever.

SOLDIER: God's curse on those filthy heathen!

PERCY (his teeth clenched with pain): And twice be cursed this foul land of ruin and misery!

HUNT (frowning): How did the savages manage to breach the wall before an alarm could be sounded by the sentries, Master Percy?

7

PERCY (*with a contemptuous toss of his head in the* SOLDIER's *direction*): Ask our brave warrior there. He was on sentry duty.

SOLDIER (*defensively*): I was stationed at the west wall, sir! 'Twas the east wall they breached.

PERCY: Could you not have fired your musket to alarm the garrison?

SOLDIER (*grumbles*): Aye, and hold in my hand an empty weapon and be at the mercy of those painted devils? 'Twas only by God's providence I was able to find safety here, for my way was barred to the blockhouse.

HUNT (*standing up, finished with* PERCY): I'm afraid that will have to do for the time being, Master Percy. (*Stoops to pick up from the floor the arrow he had extracted from* PERCY's *leg*) Hmm . . . God's mercy it was only your leg. (*Turns aside and looks toward the window with a sad shake of his head*) I fear to think what may have been the fate of those poor souls guarding the east wall . . . when the savages . . . (*He shakes his head in concern.*)

PERCY (*after a pause, with bitter despondency*): What matters when, where, or how we all perish, Mr. Hunt? (*With a motion toward* BROWN) That poor misbegotten wretch there, taken by the plague that has carried off so many of us . . . what matters where a miserable soul such as he perishes? He'll stink no less here than he would in some slimy, befouled gutter in Billingsgate.

HUNT (*with some sternness*): Master Percy, humble as he is, his soul is just as precious in the eyes of the Lord as yours and mine.

(*He walks up to the altar and bows his head, prepared to pray.*)

PERCY (*low, not to* HUNT): Aye, pray, good Mr. Hunt. Pray that the Lord in heaven—if there be one—pray that He deliver us from this hell . . . this slaughterhouse . . . this forsaken, howling wilderness, even if it be to a shallow pit in the ground.

HUNT (*praying*): Oh, Almighty God, save and deliver us, we humbly beseech thee, from the hands of our enemies; that

we, being armed with Thy defense, may be preserved ever-
more from all perils, to glorify Thee, who art the only
giver of all victory; through the merits of Thy son, Jesus
Christ, our Lord. Amen. (*He turns from the altar, steps
down from the dais, looks at each one in turn, shakes his
head sadly.*) I prayed to the Lord for deliverance from our
enemies, Master Percy. But, like a poor actor, who mouths
a well-rehearsed line merely by rote, my mind, my thoughts
—may God forgive me—were far away in England . . .
England. (*Pauses as he looks off into the distance.*) I
recalled, as if it were yesterday, how we stood on deck,
taking a last look at England as the vessel swung to the
tide in the moment of departure for the New World. The
gallants in silks and satins—(PERCY *looks down at his own
tattered clothes with a wry smile.*)—Dissipated men of
the world, still smelling of the stews and grog shops of
London, in which they had spent their fortunes. A few
sober gentlemen—aye, all too few—standing apart from
the others. (*Looking at* PERCY *meaningfully*) A younger
son or two of the great nobility . . . standing apart from
the others. (*Looking at* SOLDIER, *who is intent on the
scene outside the window*) A number of hard-bitten
soldiers, eager to use their swords in carving out a fortune
in the New World . . . standing apart from the others.
(*Looks at* BROWN, *who is now cupping his two hands, as
if holding something in his palms*) And some plain working people, artisans and laborers. All too few. All too few
. . . standing as a group apart, prudently keeping out of
the way of their betters. (*He looks about sadly at the
three.*) And as I look at you this morning, I can see that
this then is the cause of your ruin . . . your undoing. This
standing apart one from the other . . . one from the other.
 (*From offstage comes the distant sound of cannon
fire.*)
SOLDIER (*elated*): The vessel! The vessel in the river is turning cannon fire upon the savages!
PERCY (*scowls*): What do the fools expect to do? Drop their
shots within the stockade? Like as not they will kill as

many of our company as Indians.

SOLDIER(*elated*): Hah, no! The vessel is firing over the top of the fort to frighten the savages away! And how they run! The roar of the guns was enough to send them scurrying back into the forest!

(*The* SOLDIER *leaves the window and starts to remove the barricade from the door.*)

PERCY: Hold, you blasted idiot! (SOLDIER *stops.*) We must wait for the bells in the fort to sound for safety before 'tis prudent to expose ourselves! They are treacherous, these heathen . . .

BROWN (*his eyes bright with fever, cupping his hands*): Gold . . . Gold. Look, ye, gold. (*With awe*) More plentiful in Virginia than copper be in England . . .

PERCY (*with a bitter, disgusted laugh*): Aye, gold! Hah, even the dripping-pans and the chamber pots of the savages are wrought in pure gold, and studded with rubies and diamonds! (*Mutters pityingly*) Poor gullible wretch!

BROWN (*eagerly, taking* PERCY *literally*): Aye, rubies and diamonds! The savage Indians—they go forth on their holy days and gather 'em by the seashore, to hang on their children's coats . . .

PERCY (*with deep self-disgust*): By the blood of Saint Joseph! (*Broodingly, low*) Fools! Fools! Wretched fools! And none a greater fool than George Percy himself.

(BROWN *has taken a leaflet from inside his jerkin. He extends it to* HUNT *with a pathetic, pleading look.*)

BROWN: Good Mr. Hunt . . . Your reverence . . . please, sir. Read nor write can I, sir. Doth not it note herein that what I say be true indeed . . . about the gold, diamonds and . . . and rubies?

(HUNT *walks up to* BROWN, *takes the leaflet from his hand. His face turns grim as he reads it.*)

PERCY: Like as not one of those lying handbills printed by the London Company to raise men and money for this venture . . . this venture into darkness. (HUNT *nods.* PERCY *extends his hand for it.*) If you please, Mr. Hunt. (HUNT *walks over to* PERCY *and, with a sigh, hands it to* him. PERCY *glances at it.*) Ah, yes. This one I have seen. (*With a snort*) Hah! Mark this! (*Reads, with a flourish*) "The land of Virginia in the New World is like unto the Promised Land as described by Moses. But, flowing not with milk, but with pearls. Dripping not with honey, but with gold. E'en the very sands on the shores of Virginia gleam bright with diamonds, and . . . (*He crumples the leaflet, and, with fierce disgust, flings it in a ball towards* BROWN.) Pah!

(BROWN, *his eyes on the leaflet, drags his body painfully towards it.*)

BROWN: Pearls . . . gold. It does then indeed note that. (*Smooths out the leaflet on the floor. He looks up at* HUNT *imploringly, begging to be told a lie.*) In truth, doth it not say that, Reverend Sir?

(PERCY *is looking at* HUNT *with a tight, sardonic smile.*)

HUNT (*with angry indignation*): Aye, it does indeed say that, you poor, misguided soul! But not in truth! Aye, not in truth! They lied, these worshipers of Mammon! These false prophets of Baal! (*Turns away*) May God have mercy on their souls when comes their day of judgment.

BROWN (*shaking his head, dazed; speaking as one who finds it hard to face the truth*) No gold . . . no pearls . . . no rubies? They . . . they lied, Reverend Sir? Your worship . . . they lied?

(HUNT *walks over to* BROWN *and helps him back to his pallet.*)

HUNT: Come, now, rest quietly or you might bring on another blood flux. There, now, lie still . . . lie still, good man.

PERCY (*more in pity than contempt*): Poor soul. Poor misguided wretch.

(*The* SOLDIER *through all this has remained stationed at the window, seemingly quite removed and indifferent to what was being said. Now he turns his head and speaks to* PERCY, *with as much impudence as he dares in speaking to the gentry.*)

SOLDIER (*with a slight sneer*): And you, your worship?

(PERCY *has not heard his words. He turns his head slowly toward the* SOLDIER.)

PERCY: Did you speak, soldier?

SOLDIER: Aye. (*Hesitates*) Your pardon, Master Percy—but what brought your honor to this God-forsaken wilderness?

PERCY (*scowling*): Gold, soldier. Gold.

SOLDIER (*with a mocking lift to his brow*): Ah, indeed . . . even as that poor wretch there, Edward Brown?

PERCY: Aye, even as that poor wretch there, Edward Brown.

SOLDIER: You believed the stories about the riches to be found on these shores? And you an educated gentleman?

(PERCY *begins to laugh mirthlessly. He stops short and winces with pain as he clutches his leg.*)

PERCY (*tightly*): Nay, soldier, I no more believed there was gold to be found on these shores than did the worthy directors of the London Company who spawned this venture.

SOLDIER (*regarding* PERCY *with puzzlement*): No? But, did you not just say . . . ?

PERCY: Nay. Neither gold from mines, nor gold to be filched from the poor heathen who have it not. (*Nods grimly*) But gold there be. And 'tis known full well where and how to garner it.

(*The* SOLDIER *moves up to* PERCY *with anger and menace.* PERCY *regards him with cold scorn, but places his hand on the hilt of his sword.* HUNT, *in apprehension, steps between them.*)

HUNT: Come, come, soldier; he but teases you.

SOLDIER (*paying* HUNT *no heed, demanding*): You, Master Percy—do you know where this treasure can be found?

PERCY: Aye, I know where it can be found.

(*The* SOLDIER *shoulders* HUNT *aside and glares down at* PERCY.)

SOLDIER: By the blood! if ye highborn gentlemen think ye can cheat us out of our share—

(*At this point* BROWN, *who has been staring at the leaflet on the floor beside his pallet, suddenly begins to shout and pound the leaflet with his two clenched fists.*)

BROWN (*with maddened vehemence*): Lies! Lies! Lies! All lies! A black curse on their heads!

(*He is stopped by a spasm of coughs and choked sobs. HUNT rushes over and kneels down beside him.*)

HUNT: Come now, Edward Brown; calm yourself, do! (*He gently forces him down.*) Stop that, now!

(*PERCY is ignoring the SOLDIER, who stands over him threateningly. PERCY's eyes are on BROWN, showing pity.*)

SOLDIER: Where is this treasure to be gotten, I ask ye!

PERCY (*swinging around to him fiercely*): From the seas, you bloody fool! From the seas!

SOLDIER (*puzzled*): What say you?

PERCY: Aye, from the ships that sail the Spanish Main!

(*At this, HUNT looks up toward PERCY. The SOLDIER, with a shrug and a puzzled frown, walks back to the window. HUNT, after covering BROWN with the blanket, walks up to PERCY and regards him severely.*)

HUNT: What mean you by that remark, sir?

PERCY (*suddenly*): Nothing, Mr. Hunt, nothing.

HUNT (*sorrowfully*): Then 'twas true, what I heard.

PERCY: What was true, sir?

HUNT: That the prime purpose of this venture was to establish a base for freebooting upon the high seas.

PERCY: Freebooting? Not necessarily so, Mr. Hunt. To proceed against vessels at war with England . . . ?

HUNT (*interrupting sharply*): Aye, and before long, Heaven help any vessel, flying any colors, once that is started. So it has always been proven, has it not, Master Percy? (*PERCY turns his eyes away with a shrug of his shoulders.*) And you would knowingly lend yourself . . . your noble name, to such a sinful venture?

PERCY (*with a bitter laugh*): My noble name indeed!

HUNT: As a son of the Earl of Northumberland, have you not a responsibility?

PERCY: Responsibility? To whom, I pray you?

HUNT: To yourself. (*As PERCY is mute*) Don't you care what

happens to you?

PERCY: Nay, I care not a whit what happens to me. Just as no one cares a whit what becomes of me. Least of all my esteemed father, the Earl of Northumberland.

HUNT (*placing his hand on* PERCY's *shoulder*): I care for you, my son. For you, and all ye poor sinners thrown together on these shores. (*He walks away. Turns to look sadly down on* BROWN.)

PERCY (*looking toward* BROWN): Everyone, and everything, comes to naught in the end, aye, sir?

HUNT (*without turning*): The ill conceived and ill ventured always do come to naught.

PERCY: In truth, you, too, have been cheated in this venture, have you not, Mr. Hunt?

HUNT: Cheated? Of what, I pray you?

PERCY (*with a wry smile*): Of souls. Aye, we of gold and you of souls. (*As* HUNT *turns away with a frown*) For did you not come here to bring the heathen into the Kingdom of God, and save their souls from everlasting darkness? (HUNT *remains silent, his expression grim.*) Tell me, Mr. Hunt, how many of the heathen have you converted to Christianity?

HUNT (*swinging around, resentfully*): None! Nor is it any wonder, when ye have made the name of Christ Jesus hateful to them! Ravaging their stores! Burning their villages! Murdering their people! (*Sorrowfully*) And this, after they had extended a hand of friendship to us. Can you blame them for feeling naught but murder and rage toward us? There's little enough to commend ourselves to them as Christians, unless we learn to behave as such.

SOLDIER: 'Tis true, your Reverence, we did seize their corn. But, mind you, it was after they refused to barter it for . . .

HUNT (*interrupting scathingly*): For glass beads and trinkets! When their winter supply of corn meant life or death to their people!

SOLDIER (*sullenly*): What would you have us do, sir . . . perish from starvation?

HUNT: Plant! Plant your own corn!

14

(Percy *looks down at his palms with a quizzical smile,
as if to say,* "What, with these hands?")
Soldier (*scornfully*): I am a soldier, sir! Not a peasant
clod!
Hunt (*with more sorrow than reproof*): Soldiers . . . gentlemen . . . merchants. Aye, even hairdressers, perfumers and
goldsmiths. Adventurers all. Spending your time in a vain
search for gold. All of one mind, yet all standing apart.
Soldiers, gentlemen, and commoners, divided by hate and
suspicion. (*Forebodingly.*) 'Twill be the cause of your
undoing, it will indeed.
(*The tolling of the bell is heard in the distance. It continues under following until cued out.*)
Soldier (*elated*): The bell! The savages are routed, thanks
be to God! (*He moves to door and begins to remove
benches, then turns to* Percy *with mixed feelings.*) Shall
I . . . shall I assist you to your quarters, Master Percy?
Percy (*trying to stand, speaks painfully*): If you please,
soldier.
Hunt: 'Tis best you bide here a spell, until I fetch some
dressings and attend to your wound properly.
Percy (*sinking back*): Thank you, Mr. Hunt. 'Twould be
wiser.
(*The fort bell stops at this point.* Soldier *opens the
door, knuckles his brow to them, then exits quickly.*)
Hunt: Master Percy, I did not think to ask of you before . . .
Percy: Aye, Mr. Hunt?
Hunt: What in heaven's name were you doing, wandering
about at dawn, away from the fort?
Percy (*smiles*): Ironic, isn't it, sir? (Hunt *looks at him
inquiringly.*) I was sore troubled in mind, and could not
sleep, and thought me that I would perhaps find peace
and solace in the church. And the one instant when I am
drawn to commune with the Lord . . . I, who haven't seen
the inside of a church in many a year . . . at that moment
the savages decide to attack the settlement, and—whist!
An arrow pierces my leg. (*Shakes his head with a smile*)
The Lord moves in mysterious ways indeed.

HUNT: He does indeed.

PERCY (*frowning*): Look you, sir . . . I have never made pretense of being a good Christian. (*With a rueful laugh*) In truth, Reverend, I doubt if one George Percy dare call himself a Christian at all. (*Sincerely*) But this . . . this I can attest to, sir. And none among us will deny it. (*Pauses*) We need you here, Mr. Hunt. (HUNT *looks away with a frown.*) Need you more than the people at home do. But you leave for England when the vessel sails on the morrow.

HUNT (*in conflict, doubtfully*): I trust it is the Lord's will that I return to England. My Lord Bishop has offered me the parish of Almondsbury, which has fallen vacant. And yet . . . I don't know . . .

BROWN (*weakly*): Good Mr. Hunt . . . Please, your reverence . . .

HUNT (*as he walks toward* BROWN): I don't know . . .
(HUNT *is kneeling by* BROWN'S *side, and talking to him quietly.* BROWN'S *eyes are fastened on his face pleadingly.* PERCY'S *head is bowed, his eyes cast down broodingly.*)

PERCY (*more to himself*): You will be in England in mid-May. England . . . England in mid-May . . . when the harebells and the kingcups are in bloom among the gorse in the meadow below Alnwick Castle where I first breathed the sweet air of Northumberland. Oh, how sweetly smelled the bog myrtle and the alder bush along the banks of the Aln, its waters rushing down from the Blue Cheviots to the north. (*He buries his face in his hands.*) Lord God in heaven, grant me that I see England once again.
(*He does not see* HUNT *rise, walk up toward him, and stop a short distance away.*)

HUNT (*low, with deep compassion*): Poor lad. Aye, poor children all of them. (*He walks some steps toward the altar, stops before the dais.*) Grant me the wisdom, O, Lord, to know Thy will, that I, Thy poor servant here on earth may serve Thee best. (*He turns his face half-looking towards* PERCY, *who remains in the same position, his face buried in his hands.*) Who shall take them by the hand

and lead them out of the wilderness? Who will be their teacher, their guide when I am gone? Who can show them in their strife, and in their greed, that there is one who stands above their worldly ambitions? One they can trust as a just father, as they can trust their Father in heaven. For with all their impiety, with all their trespass against God's law, they still look to me and need me as a symbol of hope and salvation. Without that, they perish.

(HUNT *turns and faces the door as he hears* CAPTAIN JOHN SMITH *calling from outside.*)

SMITH (*offstage*): Mr. Hunt! Mr. Hunt, sir! (SMITH *enters, followed by* SECOND SOLDIER.) Well, well! 'Tis indeed a great joy to see you unharmed, sir! Those bloody heathen! (*Sees* PERCY) By God's lid, Master Percy, if we didn't think you were taken by the savages and carried off to be tortured! And here ye be, b'God's providence! (*Notes his wound*) Wounded be ye? (PERCY *looks at him stonily, with evident distaste.* SMITH *looks at* BROWN.) What ails this one, Mr. Hunt?

HUNT: Taken with the sickness, Captain Smith.

SMITH (*with no warmth or sympathy*): Another one, aye? Will he . . . ? (HUNT *shakes his head sadly.*) Bad, too bad.

PERCY: Did we suffer any losses, Captain?

SMITH: None but those two bloody sentries, God burn their souls! They must have been in a drunken stupor when the savages scaled the wall. By the beard of St. Joseph, they well deserved their fate! 'Twas only by the mercy of God that we all were not tomahawked in our beds! On the morrow, Mr. Hunt, I'll see to it that every soul in the colony will be here in church to give praise for His divine mercy. And, by heaven, they'd better be here, and down on their knees, or they'll bloody well feel the flat of my sword on their backs, sir!

HUNT (*with a heavy-hearted sigh, mumbles as he regards* SMITH): And the Lord sent His angel to make straight their path to heaven.

(SMITH *hasn't caught* HUNT's *words.*)

SMITH: Eh, Mr. Hunt?

HUNT (*sighs*): Nothing, Captain Smith, nothing. But, would you do me the kindness, sir, to order one of your men to fetch my chest from the vessel and bring it back to shore?

SMITH (*flabbergasted*): What? Fetch back your . . . ?

HUNT: Aye, Captain Smith, I've decided to remain in Jamestown.

(As SMITH *looks at* HUNT, *his mouth agape,* PERCY *regards the clergyman with a comprehending smile on his face. The curtain descends slowly.*)

C U R T A I N

Mutiny on

the Mayflower

By HENRY H. WALSH

MUTINY ON THE MAYFLOWER

CHARACTERS: 17 identifiable males,
as many extras as required
for production purposes;
2 females, 2 or 3 extras

PLAYING TIME: 55 minutes

SETS: Two

❦ Historical Notes

LESS THAN ONE-THIRD of the 102 passengers on the *Mayflower* were of the Holland group. The rest were poor people, humble farmers, laborers, and artisans, picked up in London and elsewhere in England, some of them belonging to the outlawed religious band, the Brownists. A more courageous party never sailed from England to venture into the dark, unknown wilderness across the Atlantic. But, in the eyes of the Bishop of London, they were contemptible troublemakers . . . "instructed by guides (the Holland group) fit for them, cobblers, tailors, feltmakers, and such like trash."

They started out from Southampton in two vessels, but the *Speedwell*, the other vessel provided by the syndicate, was so rotten and leaky they had to make back to port. Some of the passengers were so discouraged by this time that they withdrew from the venture. The rest crowded into the little *Mayflower* and, at last, "all being compacte togeather in one shipe" they sailed from Plymouth, England, in September. That enforced delay was to prove heartbreakingly fateful in the months to come.

Early in November they found themselves within sight of land, far to the north, and beyond the limits of the Virginia Company patent. After extensive explorations within the region of Cape Cod—under the leadership of Captain Miles Standish—they chose a site for their settlement, and the landing at Plymouth was made on December 21, 1620.

But, even before they came ashore on November 11 to begin their "discoveries," they stopped to consider their situation. For, having no charter of their own to define their rights and responsibilities as individuals, and being beyond the jurisdiction of the Virginia Company and English law, they felt the need before disembarking to draw up a covenant to be signed by all, providing for a simple form of government under which officers were to be elected and laws enacted. This was the famous "Mayflower Pact." They were not idle words. The leaders who drafted it were people with a deep sense of community, forged and welded together by persecution, bitter hardships, alienation from their fatherland and the body of English society, and, because of their profound religious convictions, at odds with the Established Church of England.

But the question keeps arising in the minds of historians: why did they not continue south to Virginia? Did they prefer the bleak, forbidding coast of Cape Cod to the pleasant, fertile lands to the south? Some history books state that the landing at Cape Cod was a matter of pure chance—a navigational error. Others, that they ran into dangerous shoals and feared to venture any farther. But, then, again, Bradford in his *History of the Plymouth Plantation* definitely states that the intention was to settle in the Dutch territory along the Hudson River after they left England. In the play, the author has explored the mystery of the *Mayflower*, and, after extensive research, drawn the conclusion that the Plymouth landing was not a matter of mere chance, but a well-calculated decision to settle beyond the jurisdiction of the Virginia Company, the Crown, and the Bishops of England. For only so could they be truly free.

ᛉ Production Notes

❨ Characters

WILLIAM BRADFORD, age 31, one of the brethren, a leader of the Plymouth venture. Second Governor of Plymouth

DEACON JOHN CARVER, age 60, first Governor of Plymouth

WILLIAM BREWSTER, age 65, the oldest member of the brethren

CAPTAIN CHRISTOPHER JONES, captain of the Mayflower

FIRST SAILOR

EDWARD BROWNE, passenger, one of the "Strangers"

WOMAN, an offstage voice

MILES STANDISH, military leader of the colony

MATE of the vessel, voice offstage

BO'SN of the Mayflower

DOROTHY BRADFORD, William Bradford's wife

PRISCILLA MULLINS, age 19, daughter of William Mullins, "Stranger"

SECOND SAILOR, crewman

THIRD SAILOR, crewman

BRETHREN, a collective term to define the devout and deeply committed members of the colony who came from Holland, the "Saints." Onstage: EDWARD WINSLOW, ISAAC ALLERTON, DEACON FULLER, FRANCIS COOKE, MOSES FLETCHER and CHRISTOPHER MARTIN

SETTLERS, a general term for the passengers at large

JOHN ALDEN, "hired hand," on year's contract

WILLIAM TREVORE, "hired hand," a mariner by profession

JOHN BILLINGTON, "Stranger" . . . "Ye most profane man in the colony"

STEPHEN HOPKINS, "Stranger"

23

LEISTER, *indentured servant to Hopkins*
DOTEY, *also indentured to Hopkins*
SAILORS, *as extras, three in number*
WILLIAM MULLINS, *"Stranger" . . . Priscilla's father*
WOMEN, *three or four in number, as extras*
TOM TINKER, *"Stranger"*
FIRST SETTLER, *offstage voice*
SECOND SETTLER, *offstage voice*

❲ **Scenes**

SCENE 1: *A cabin on the Mayflower, the morning of November 11, 1620.*
SCENE 2: *The midship deck on the Mayflower, the afternoon of the same day.*

❲ **Settings**

SCENE 1: A cabin on the Mayflower. The light enters from a mullioned window up center. Below the window a desk and chair. A bunk bed, sea chest and a locker in the far right hand corner. A table and chair down center. Entrance is at upper left. SCENE 2: The midships deck of the vessel. The base of a mast rises from the deck down right center. A few feet left of the mast is a canvas covered hatch, rising a foot or so off the deck. The portside rail runs parallel with the deck backstage. The lower part of the shrouds and ratlines are outlined sharply against a grey sky.

❲ **Costumes**

SCENE 1: Bradford, Carver and Brewster wear the costumes of the "Pilgrims" so familiar to us in illustration. The broad-brimmed, high-crowned hat is worn by Bradford, but Carver and Brewster wear black skull caps. They wear doublets with turned-back white cuffs and flat white collars, pantaloons tied below the knee, stockings and buckled shoes. Dorothy Bradford and Priscilla wear long gowns with turned-back white cuffs and collars, and on their heads muslin caps covered with shawls. Miles Standish is in the military costume of England in the early 17th century: metal helmet, short surcoat worn over wide-sleeved shirt, pantaloons tucked into turned-down boots. A sword hangs from a wide belt carried over his shoulder. The seamen wear costumes resembling the dress of pirates: colorful bandannas covering their heads, neckerchiefs around their throats, short-sleeved collarless shirts, wide pantaloons, open below the knee, that look like short skirts, stockings and short boots. A broad belt around the waist holds a sheathed knife. Captain Jones' clothing is not very different from that of the civilians, except for a broad belt or sash around his waist that holds a pistol. He wears a long black cloak over his clothing. In Scene 2 the passengers are dressed like Bradford, but many of them are quite ragged in appearance. Most wear long cloaks over their shoulders.

❲ Properties

SCENE 1: Desk, table, three chairs, bunk bed, footlocker and sea chest. A cat-'o-nine-tails hangs from a peg. An inkpot and quill on the desk. A parchment map on the table. Some sheets of heavy parchment writing paper.

SCENE 2: A coil of rope and a wooden bucket.

❲ Lighting

SCENE 1: Morning daylight streaming in through window.

SCENE 2: After daylight on a cloudy, bleak day.

Scene II – "mutiny on the mayflower"

Mutiny on
the Mayflower

SCENE 1

A cabin on the Mayflower, anchored off the coast of Cape Cod on the bleak morning of November 11, 1620. Light enters from a mullioned window set in a slanting wall up center. To the right of the window is a desk and chair. In the far right corner of the cabin are a bunk bed and sea chest. A long cloak and high crowned hat hang from a peg near the bed. Down center are a chair and a table on which a parchment map is spread flat. A big Bible anchors down one corner of the map. The entrance to the cabin is at upper left.

At curtain rise DEACON JOHN CARVER is seated at the table up center studying the map intently. WILLIAM BRADFORD is standing at the window with his back to the audience gazing morosely across the water to the shore beyond. He turns his head to speak to CARVER.

BRADFORD: In heaven's name, Deacon Carver, what is that God-forsaken land of sand and rock called?
    (CARVER moves his finger, which stops at a point on the map.)
CARVER: If this map is truly accurate, we are anchored here,

at Cape Harbor, off the shores of Cape Cod.

(BRADFORD *glances out of the window again.*)

BRADFORD (*gloomily*): Cape Cod, is it? (*As he turns and walks towards* CARVER.) 'Twould have been far better named Cape Nod, the land that God gave to Cain when he drove him forth east from Eden.

CARVER (*looking up*): Perhaps the Lord in His infinite wisdom placed His hand on the helm, to steer us to a shore beyond the jurisdiction of the Crown and the Anglican Bishops of England, where we can worship in freedom and glorify His name like true Christians, William.

BRADFORD: But, deacon, are we not far north of the 41st parallel?

CARVER (*with a glance down at the map, murmurs*): We are indeed.

BRADFORD (*worried*): Then without the sanction of the Crown we have no legal right to settle here.

CARVER (*solemnly*): Should we bow to the legal judgment of King James, or the divine will of God, Master Bradford?

BRADFORD (*with a shake of his head*): Aye, 'tis very well when you speak for us, the brethren, deacon. But we are but a mere few among the one hundred and three souls—men, women and children all—who sailed with us from England. What of the Strangers . . . and the servants . . . and the hired hands? (*With a sigh, he motions towards the window.*) How can we say to those poor travel-weary people that this is their new home, their Promised Land? With no friends to welcome them when they step ashore. No towns or houses to shelter them from the cold, bitter winds of winter that are nigh upon us.

CARVER (*with some doubt*): But as good Christian souls, will they not agree . . .

BRADFORD (*interrupting gently*): Deacon Carver, I doubt if they care too much under whom, or how, they worship, if they can live in peace and better their estate here on earth. (*Motions towards the window dolefully*) And that will not be to their liking. Nay, not to their liking at all, when it was their belief we were bound for the Virginia colony.

(*Direfully*) The good Lord only knows what they will say, or do, if they are told . . . (*He stops as* CAPTAIN CHRISTOPHER JONES, *master of the* Mayflower, *enters scowling. He is followed closely by* WILLIAM BREWSTER. BRADFORD *looks at* JONES *intently.*) Well, Captain Jones?

JONES: We daren't attempt it, Master Bradford.

BRADFORD: But we must! We must try again to make our way to the Dutch settlements on the Hudson River!

BREWSTER: Aye, if at all possible. Otherwise . . .

JONES (*interrupts curtly*): But we did try! . . . and almost got wrecked on the shoals a day's sail from here. 'Twas only b'God's mercy we were able to come about and make our way back. (*With a scowl, he points to the map.*) If Captain John Smith's map there had given some marking of the soundings . . .

BREWSTER: But when the wind and weather are more favorable . . .

JONES: Master Brewster, I cannot afford to tarry much longer. My food and supplies are hardly sufficient to carry me and my crew home to England again . . . even on half rations, sir! (*Grumbles*) If we had departed Southampton in mid-August as we had planned, and not lay to in port for a long month, consuming our food . . .

BREWSTER: But how could we have foreseen the mishaps which delayed our departure?

JONES: 'Twas not of my doing, sir!

BREWSTER (*mollifyingly*): Nor did I say it was, Captain Jones.

(BRADFORD *has been studying the map intently.*)

BRADFORD: Captain, if we were to journey a few leagues eastward, and so avoid the shoals . . . then come about and bear southwards again . . .

JONES (*interrupts*): Master Bradford, I beg of you, listen to me. (*He pauses, then continues ominously.*) I just came from a talk with my bo'sn . . . (*He nods in* BREWSTER's *direction*) and Master Brewster can bear me out in that, he was there . . . My bo'sn has warned me—and he, more so than I, knows the mood in the foc's'l—if I were to give orders for anchor up and away to the southwards, I would have a mutiny on my hands!

CARVER (*disbelievingly*): Oh, come now, Captain Jones . . . 'tis hard to credit that, sir.

(BRADFORD *is looking at* JONES *narrowly*.)

JONES (*irritated*): Surely you are not unaware of the ill feeling that exists between your passengers and my crew?

BRADFORD (*grimly*): And 'tis no wonder, sir! Your mariners are a most unruly and profane lot! They have done everything possible to add to the misery of our poor people from the day we sailed from Southampton.

(JONES *regards* BRADFORD *for a moment before answering, an element of malicious satisfaction in the slight smile on his lips*.)

JONES: Oh, yes, they are indeed a profane lot, as you say. To be sure, the light of sweet charity and brotherly love does not burn as brightly in their hearts as it does in yours, sir. For they live by, and respect but one law . . . the lash! But, even so, they are as human as all mortals be when facing disaster: they look to their own survival—and trust the Lord to look to the Godly.

CARVER (*sadly*): Our Savior died on the cross for all humanity, sir. He made no distinction between . . .

(CARVER *stops abruptly at a commotion starting offstage. There seems to be a fight going on. There are cries, curses and the stamp of feet on the deck: all the sounds indicating a violent scuffle in progress. The words are mainly indistinguishable, topping each other, but some come through. The men in the cabin are immobile for a moment, then* JONES *rushes for the exit*.)

JONES: By the beard of St. Joseph, what's a-foot now!

(*He exits left, with* BRADFORD, BREWSTER *and* CARVER *following him. The stage is empty for the moment. There are voices on deck*.)

BROWNE (*offstage*): You swine of the sea! I'll have your heart's blood for that!

WOMAN (*frantically*): For the love of God, stop them! Stop them!

FIRST SAILOR: Damn ye to hell, you . . . (*He stops abruptly as there is the sound of the lash and* JONES' *voice offstage.*)
JONES: Drop it! Drop that club, I say, or I'll flay you to the bone!
BRADFORD: Drop that knife, Browne! (*There is a sharp scuffle.*)
STANDISH (*commands*): Give it me! (*Struggling*) I have it, Master Bradford!
BRADFORD: Into the cabin with him, Captain Standish!
JONES (*commands*): I'll have the deck cleared, mate!
MATE (*over the sound of the lash*): Aye! . . . Get ye forward! To the foc's'l, all of ye! (*There is a surly grumble.*)
JONES: All passengers below! Clear off the deck, I say! Bo'sn, get that louse-ridden wretch into the cabin!
BO'SN: Aye, sir!
   (*The* BO'SN *enters the cabin, pushing* FIRST SAILOR *before him roughly, taking a couple of swipes at him with a cat-o'-nine-tails meanwhile. The* SAILOR'S *face shows signs of battle, and he is snarling like an angry beast.* MILES STANDISH *appears behind them, clutching* BROWNE *by the collar as he propels him into the cabin.* BROWNE'S *forehead is streaked with blood. The* SAILOR *suddenly frees himself from the* BO'SN *and tries to get at* BROWNE.)
FIRST SAILOR: You filthy swine! I'll . . .
BO'SN: No, you don't! (*He shoves him violently away, sending him sprawling to the deck, then advances on him with the whip upraised.*) By the blood, I'll cool your choler if I have to . . . (*He stops as* JONES *enters, commanding sharply.*)
JONES: Hold it, Bo'sn! (*To* SAILOR) Up on your feet!
   (*The* SAILOR *gets to his feet, dabbing at his wound with his neckerchief as he glowers at the* BO'SN. BRADFORD, CARVER *and* BREWSTER *enter looking very disturbed.* BROWNE *points an accusing finger at the* SAILOR.)
BROWNE: Your worships, that wretched villain and others seized up my belongings and dumped them on the deck!
JONES (*glaring at the* SAILOR): Did you?

31

FIRST SAILOR: Aye, 'tis the end of their journey whether they like it or no! We will not suffer . . .

JONES (*roars*): Hold your tongue! (*Turns to Bo'sn*) Bo'sn, take him below and put him in irons! We'll deal with him later!

FIRST SAILOR (*whines*): But, captain, did you not tell the mate . . .

JONES (*sharply*): Hold your tongue, I say, or I'll add ten lashes for every word you utter!

(*The* SAILOR, *with an aggrieved glance at* JONES, *is led away by the* Bo'sn. BROWNE *appeals to the* BRETHREN.)

BROWNE: Is there any truth in what is being said? That . . . that ye mean to settle here?

BRADFORD (*hesitantly, frowns*): We have come to no final decisions where we shall settle, Peter Browne. But . . .

BROWNE: But we were bound for Virginia! (*Accusingly*) Or so we were led to believe.

JONES (*crossly*): By the saints, who knows where Virginia begins and Virginia ends!

BRADFORD (*thoughtfully*): There may be some truth in that.

BROWNE (*aghast*): But this . . . this howling wasteland, sir!

BRADFORD (*acrimoniously*): I just told you, we have made no final decision!

(BROWNE *studies the faces of the* BRETHREN *in cold silence for a moment.*)

BROWNE (*grimly*): I see.

BRADFORD: And may that suffice you until we do?

BROWNE (*tightly*): It may not, I make bold to say. (*Warningly*) And I would advise you, good sirs, you take council with the passengers all before ye act on your decision. They may feel they have a right to be consulted in the matter. (*He nods curtly.*) By your leave, good sirs.

(*He turns and exits from the cabin, with* JONES *scowling and the others following his departure with anxious expressions.*)

STANDISH (*uneasily*): He may cause trouble. (*As he walks towards exit*) I had better go below among the passengers.

BRADFORD: Deacon, perhaps 'twould be wise if you and

Elder Brewster do likewise. (BREWSTER and CARVER nod and turn to go.) And if there are signs of foment among the passengers, caution them to preserve better walking . . . for the good of all. (BREWSTER and CARVER leave.)

JONES (grinning derisively at BRADFORD): "Better walking." Sound advice, Master Bradford. I'm off to caution my crew to do the same. But, I'm afraid, those sinful sons of Satan may not understand my meaning if I put it as you do. So, I'll just caution them to watch their step . . . or else. Now that, sir, is a language they will understand. (He nods and turns to go.)

BRADFORD: Captain Jones . . .

    (JONES stops and turns to face him. BRADFORD looks at him closely.)

JONES: Aye, sir?

BRADFORD: By any chance, did you give orders to any of your crew to fetch up the passengers' belongings and deposit them on deck?

JONES (bridles): What! Most certainly not, sir! (BRADFORD looks far from convinced as he regards JONES narrowly. JONES scowls at him resentfully.) Nevertheless, sir, I can't say I was sorry it happened.

BRADFORD: Indeed?

JONES: Aye, for in that you could sense the dangerous mood of the crew, and judge for yourself what dire consequences might follow if I ordered the anchor up and sailed for Virginia . . . or even Hudson's River.

BRADFORD: Aye, that I can see. But, I can't help but wonder —and question—if the shoals that made you come about and return to this harbor were as dangerous as they, let us say, appeared to be?

JONES (his face dark with anger): Sir, I account myself a better judge of that than you! You who know little of the treacherous way of the sea and the craft of seamanship!

BRADFORD (sadly): True, I may know little of the treacherous way of the sea, or the craft of seamanship. But, I am not without knowledge of the treacherous way of man, and the craft he lives by, whether he sails upon the sea, or trods his way upon the land.

(JONES' *face twists in anger. He is about to retort, but turns away in disgust and walks towards the exit.*)

JONES (*mutters on the way out*): Bah! Bloody lot of benighted landsmen!

(BRADFORD *stands looking after him moodily, then turns and walks to the table. With a heavy sigh he seats himself, rests his elbows on the table and holds his head in his hands. He remains that way for a moment.* DOROTHY BRADFORD *enters. There is something very vague and distraught in her expression as she stops and looks at* BRADFORD *timidly. He doesn't see her as she walks toward him.*)

DOROTHY: William, good husband . . .

(BRADFORD *lifts his head with a start. He gets to his feet. There is deep sadness and pain in his eyes as he walks up to her and takes her hands in his.*)

BRADFORD: Dorothy, my dear one, you should remain below out of the damp wind, for you know you have not been too well of late.

DOROTHY: But, William, I'm terribly worried about our son (BRADFORD *sighs hopelessly at this.*) I . . . I've searched everywhere on the vessel and I can't find him.

BRADFORD (*painfully*): Oh, Dorothy . . .

DOROTHY (*continues*): And I've asked every mortal soul on board, but not a one knows where he is. And there seems to be . . . seems to be such anger and trouble among the people, I fear me he may come to harm.

BRADFORD (*placing his hands on her shoulders, tenderly*): Dorothy, dear wife, John, our son John, did not journey with us. (DOROTHY *just stares at* BRADFORD *blankly, as if his words do not penetrate her consciousness.*) Try to recall; do, dear one. How he remained behind in Holland in the care of our good friend, John Robinson. And I promise you, dear, that as soon as we are settled in safety and build us a home, we will send for him. And God willing . . .

DOROTHY (*plaintively*): William, I do wish you would

speak to him. For, I've told him time and time again not to climb up those ratlines. He may fall and injure himself sorely. Aye, 'twas only this morning I had to scold him sharply for not minding me closely. (*Vaguely*) Aye, this very morning . . .

BRADFORD (*with a heavy sigh*): Dorothy, it was not our little son you scolded so. Was I not there? It was Richard More, the lad that Elder Brewster took from the London orphanage before we departed England. (*As* DOROTHY *just stares at him blankly,* BRADFORD, *despite himself, can't help showing impatience.*) Now listen to me, Dorothy. You must try to remember. Don't you recall the hour we departed from Delshaven . . . when we were waving farewell to our lad . . . just before the seamen hauled in the gangway? (DOROTHY *begins to show some response, nods slightly.*)

DOROTHY (*slowly*): Aye . . . Aye, John Robinson was holding him up in his arms . . . the better to see us.

BRADFORD (*encouraged, with some eagerness*): That's right, dear . . . standing below on the wharf among our kind friends who had come to bid us godspeed.

(*With a growing sense of reality,* DOROTHY *begins to relive in her mind the scene as he describes it. Her eyes open wider as she gazes off into the distance. Her face begins to quiver with suffering.*)

DOROTHY (*low*): Yes . . . yes . . . he struggled so in the arms of John Robinson . . . sobbing. (*Her voice begins to rise, and she speaks more quickly.*) Sobbing as if his very heart would burst asunder in his little breast! And then he broke free . . . ran towards the gangway . . . tried to reach us before they could pull it in! (*Her voice rises higher.*) Sobbing and screaming! Screaming, "Don't leave me, mother! Mother, don't leave me!"

BRADFORD (*pleads*): Dorothy, please! Please don't distress yourself so! We will send for him soon! Soon!

DOROTHY (*continues unheeding, bitterly*): William, William, how could you stand there so cruelly, and watch John Robinson drag him off the gangway, and hear him cry, "Father! Father, take me with you! (DOROTHY *sobs*.) Please! Please take me with you!" (*She breaks down into deep sobs.* BRADFORD, *in desperation, begins to shake her slightly.*)

BRADFORD: Stop that now! Stop it, I say! (DOROTHY *starts to pound his chest with her clenched fists.*)

DOROTHY: 'Twas cruel! Cruel! Why did we leave him behind? Why? Why? Why? (*Then she leans her head on his chest and sobs.*) Our little lad! Our poor, poor child! We shall never see him again! Never! Never! (BRADFORD *strokes her hair tenderly, tries to comfort and reassure her.*)

BRADFORD: Nonsense, Dorothy, nonsense. He will be with us as soon as we are established. I promise you . . . soon . . . soon.

(PRISCILLA MULLINS *comes hurrying in at this moment. She is anxious and breathless, but her concern gives way to relief on seeing* DOROTHY *in* BRADFORD's *arms. She drops her eyes contritely.*)

PRISCILLA: I'm sorry, Master Bradford. I had to leave her side to attend Catherine Carver's maidservant who is took with the ships fever. I did ask Rose Standish to . . . to stay with her. (BRADFORD *steps back from* DOROTHY, *smiles down at her.*)

BRADFORD: You have been more than kind, Priscilla, lass. But, as you can see, my good wife is better, much better in mind now.

PRISCILLA (*sighs*): It has been such a long wearisome voyage, sir. Penned up below for more than ninety days, some of us, in those dark, noisome quarters. 'Tis a wonder, indeed, that more of us haven't become . . . (*Stops*) deeply despondent in mind. (*Pleads*) 'Twould indeed be a blessing, sir, if we were permitted to go ashore, if but to wash our filthy clothing and refresh our bodies.

(DOROTHY *has walked away to seat herself in the chair. Her hands are folded in her lap, her eyes cast down.* BRADFORD *is unaware of her relapse from reality again. But* PRISCILLA *casts an anxious glance in her direction.*)

BRADFORD: Perhaps we shall do just that, lass. (*Resigned*

sigh) It may be all for the best at that. (*Turns to* DOROTHY) Go with Priscilla, love. Go with Priscilla, and do try to seek some rest.

DOROTHY (*rising dutifully like a child*): Yes, William. (*She walks to* PRISCILLA *who places her arm around her shoulder with a gentle smile.*) But, first, Priscilla must help me find John. (*Pleadingly*) You will, won't you, Priscilla dear?

BRADFORD (*cries out in despair*): For the love of God, Dorothy! (*He drops his arms hopelessly by his side as* DOROTHY *turns slowly to face him, her eyes blank, her manner apathetic.*)

DOROTHY (*dully*): Yes, husband?

BRADFORD (*deeply discouraged*): Nothing, Dorothy . . . nothing.

(PRISCILLA *is looking toward* BRADFORD *as she leads* DOROTHY *toward the exit.* BRADFORD *motions her to him.* PRISCILLA *stops, walks up to him, while* DOROTHY *waits in a trance-like state.*)

PRISCILLA: Yes, Master Bradford?

BRADFORD (*low, gravely*): Stay close by her side, Priscilla. Don't leave her for a moment, lest she do herself injury.

PRISCILLA: You have my promise, sir.

BRADFORD: Bless you, child. (*As* PRISCILLA *walks back to* DOROTHY, *he places his hand over his eyes and murmurs prayerfully.*) Lord God in heaven, in thy abounding mercy, preserve her. (*He drops his hand.*) Aye, and preserve us all.

(*As* PRISCILLA *and* DOROTHY *reach the exit,* BREWSTER *and* CARVER *appear. They step aside to permit the two women to leave, following their departure with deep sympathy written on their faces. They walk up to* BRADFORD.)

BREWSTER: Our people demand an immediate answer, William . . . do we intend sailing for Virginia or no?

BRADFORD: (*benumbed with misery*): What did you tell them?

BREWSTER: Pray, what could I tell them? How could I explain to them at this crucial moment why we were forced

37

to change our plans on the very day we sailed from England?

CARVER: Alas, they would not have believed us, William. As it was, we were met with angry tumult and mutinous speeches.

BREWSTER: And threats, dire threats.

BRADFORD (bitterly): And now we find ourselves with no choice but to remain here! Were any mortals ever faced with such an impossible dilemma?

CARVER (with a rueful smile): Aye, Moses, for one . . . when the children of Israel murmured against him, and said, "Wherefore hast thou brought us up out of Egypt, to kill us and our children. . . ." And Moses cried unto the Lord, "What shall I do unto this people? . . . they are ready almost to stone me."

BRADFORD: If they are to behave as children, then they must be treated as children, with firmness and authority!

CARVER: Would that be wise, William? Even in settled communities, autocratic governors oft bring ruin upon themselves and their people. How much more so in the raising of a new commonwealth, where the mortar is scarcely set and the walls unbound.

BRADFORD: But there must be some authority! For if anarchy prevails among us we will all perish in the wilderness! As it is, God will have to work a miracle, considering how little food we have to see us through the long winter to come.

CARVER: What did Moses do in like situation, when faced with disunity and anarchy among the tribes he led through the wilderness?

BRADFORD (with a wry smile): He spake unto the Lord . . . and the Lord spake unto him. (The smile remains on his face as he abstractly opens the Bible and turns the leaves; longingly.) If only the Lord would speak unto us, and tell us what to do. (His eyes, which have remained half-seeing on the page, suddenly grow intent. He bends closer over the page. What he reads captures his attention. He

38

looks up in wonderment and awe.) The Lord has spoken unto us! (Turns back to the Bible and reads aloud.) "And the Word was made flesh and dwelt among us." (He straightens up and repeats as he looks off into the distance with an expression of revelation and exaltation on his face.) "And the Word was made flesh and dwelt among us." (He turns to the other two.) Aye, through the words of St. John He has made straight our path through the wilderness! (As CARVER and BREWSTER keep looking at him and at each other in profound puzzlement, he hurries over to the table under the window and draws a sheet of foolscap forward. He seats himself, dips the quill into the inkpot and looks at BREWSTER.) Come, my good friend, I will need your assistance in this. For 'tis you who know where to place all the wherefores and whereases that need go into a contract.

BREWSTER (puzzled): What . . . ? (His face suddenly lights up with dawning comprehension. But CARVER is frowning with increased puzzlement as he looks from BREWSTER to BRADFORD.)

CARVER: What in the name of all the saints is he talking about?

BREWSTER (smiling at BRADFORD): Ah, yes . . . But first we must determine who is the party of the first part.

BRADFORD (solemnly): Who else but the Lord himself, Elder.

BREWSTER: And the party of the second part?

BRADFORD: His children of course.

BREWSTER (with a smile): And we, William?

BRADFORD (with an answering smile): The Lord's advocates, shall we say?

(CARVER is still lost in puzzlement as BREWSTER walks up to BRADFORD.)

SCENE 2

The midships deck of the Mayflower on the afternoon of the same day. The base of the mainmast rises from the deck down right center. *A few feet in front of the mast is a covered, battened-down hatch which rises a foot or so off the deck. The portside rail runs parallel with the deck backstage. The lower part of the shrouds and ratlines rise from the outer side of the rail and are sharply outlined against a grey sky.*

At curtain rise SECOND SAILOR, *down center, is coiling a length of rope around his palm and elbow.* THIRD SAILOR *enters from up left carrying a wooden bucket and a scoop. He walks to the rail, appears to empty the bucket into the sea.*

SECOND SAILOR: What's afoot in the lower aft, Cordy? (*Sneering*) Just saw a covey of the holy brethren go into the cabin with the master.

THIRD SAILOR (*scowling*): Could be they got their saintly heads together, trying to make up their minds one way or t'other.

SECOND SAILOR: Ain't no t'other about it! This is where they get off, whether they like it or not!

(THIRD SAILOR *looks off toward the shore.*)

THIRD SAILOR (*with a gleeful snort*): Hah! Their promised land! Just flowing with milk and honey like the Good Book says.

SECOND SAILOR (*scowls*): And no beer?

THIRD SAILOR (*grins*): Book don't say.

SECOND SAILOR (*growls*): More's the pity. We've broached our last keg!

THIRD SAILOR (*appalled*): Nooo!

SECOND SAILOR (*dismally*): Aye, that's what the bo'sn says.

THIRD SAILOR (*outraged*): By the blood of the Savior, what would the master have us drink?

SECOND SAILOR: Water! (*Spits on deck*) Foul, stinkin' water!

THIRD SAILOR: Christ Jesus, we'll all die of the scourge with no beer to sustain us on the long voyage home!

SECOND SAILOR (*glumly*): Aye, a black curse on all their pious heads. We should have . . .

(MILES STANDISH *enters from upstage right. He marches*

*left across the deck with an eyes-front, military tread.
As he walks by* THIRD SAILOR, *the seaman, with a
derisive grin, begins to beat on the bucket with the
scoop, keeping time with* STANDISH'S *footsteps.* STAND-
ISH *stops in his tracks, wheels around, his face dark with
anger.* THIRD SAILOR *deposits the bucket on the deck,
plants his feet apart, and, with a mocking grin, leans forward belligerently, his fists clenched on his hips, inviting trouble to assuage his sense of grievance.)*

STANDISH: May ye be double-damned, you misbegotten son
of a slut!
  (THIRD SAILOR *reaches down for the bucket and begins
  to advance on* STANDISH *threateningly. But he stops when*
  STANDISH *places his hand on the hilt of his sword.)*

THIRD SAILOR: Brave, aren't ye, with that weapon to hand,
aye, Captain Shrimp?

STANDISH (*with deep disgust*): Your insults offend me no
more than those gull droppings on the deck, for they are
of the same nature. (*Wrathfully now*) But may God
strike you . . . you and those cowardly crewmen who have
seen fit to bedevil the lives of those poor souls below!
Those hapless men, women and children, compacted together like salt cod in a barrel, enduring cold, damp, and
hunger in the darkness of the hold through endless day
and endless night! (STANDISH *turns to include* SECOND
SAILOR *in his tirade.*) Is there not a modicum of Christian
kindness in your hearts to give some thought to their
misery and suffering? Need ye add to it?

SECOND SAILOR: Be damned to them! Do they spare a
thought for us? Us mariners who risk life and limb, day
upon day, scrambling through the rigging mid raging
tempest and heaving sea while they cower down below?

STANDISH (*contemptuously*): But what do you risk, but your
own miserable lives.

SECOND SAILOR (*furiously*): B'God's teeth, did you hear
that, Cordy? (*Turning on* STANDISH) So you account the
life of a seaman less than naught, do ye?

STANDISH: Nay, but you know beforehand, and full well, the

41

hazards ye face upon the sea. Even as I, a soldier, knew full well the mortal hazards I faced on the bloody field of battle in Flanders. But ye wouldn't know the courage it takes to venture forth into the unknown, leaving all that is familiar under God's light, to grope blindly in the darkness of a wild, savage land, risking not just their lives, as ye do, but the lives of those more precious than their own . . . the lives of their loved ones . . . their wives and children.

THIRD SAILOR: All the more fools they! (STANDISH *is about to retort, but, on the appearance of* JONES, *stage right, he turns away in disgust.*)

STANDISH: The likes of you wouldn't know, wouldn't understand what sets people on a course like that. For 'tis the kind of courage uncommon to your world. (*Finishes as he turns to go, mutters*) Or mine, for that matter.

(*The* SAILORS' *backs are turned to* JONES. *They are not as yet aware of his appearance on deck.* THIRD SAILOR, *still enraged by the slight, calls after* STANDISH.)

THIRD SAILOR: A black plague on all of ye! (*To* SECOND SAILOR) By the blood, I'd see them dumped ashore this very day! The . . . (*He stops on hearing* JONES.)

JONES (*sharply*): Get about your duties! (*As the* SAILORS *slink away sullenly*) And mind me now it will go hard with any one aboard this vessel who brings on further trouble! (BRADFORD, CARVER *and* BREWSTER *appear behind* JONES. *Behind them trail several of the* BRETHREN, *members of the Green Gate congregation from Holland. These are the devout and deeply committed members of the company who have come to seek religious freedom in the New World. They included* EDWARD WINSLOW, ISAAC ALLERTON, DEACON FULLER, FRANCIS COOKE, MOSES FLETCHER, *and* CHRISTOPHER MARTIN. JONES *turns to* BRADFORD *with a scowl.*)

JONES: 'Twould help no end, sir, if you could persuade your Captain Standish to keep a bridle on that fiery temper of his.

(BRADFORD *looks off in the direction of* STANDISH'*s exit.*

*He nods thoughtfully, but there is an affectionate smile
on his lips.*)
BRADFORD: A little chimney is quickly fired, Captain Jones.
But ye need have no concern on his part. Small in stature
he may be, but a great soul dwells in that body.
CARVER (*regretfully*): But I do wish he'd place some trust
in the Lord, and not all in that sword he carries.
JONES (*ominously*): Agnostic he may be, but, mark me, sirs
. . . you may very well find need for one as he, before long.
WINSLOW: I pray the Lord it prove not so.
(STANDISH *enters left with a crowd of the* SETTLERS
*behind him. They walk down center and stand in sober
silence before the* BRETHREN. *Many look ill and weak.
Most of them have anxious inquiry in their expressions.
Some are sullen; others openly hostile, standing with
folded arms. Most of the* SETTLERS *remain unseen offstage left. At times, their voices join in as they protest,
express approval, or challenge the* BRETHREN. *Some of
the women appear, but maintain a discreet distance
on the fringe of the assemblage. Among those visible
onstage are:* STANDISH, BILLINGTON, JOHN ALDEN,
BROWNE, TREVORE, MULLINS, STEPHEN HOPKINS *and his
two servants,* LEISTER *and* DOTEY, *and* TOM TINKER.
Some SAILORS, *including the* BO'SN, *are standing at the
rail, viewing the gathering with insolent smirks on their
faces.* BRADFORD *steps up on the hatch, seems to be
making a quick headcount, including the* BRETHREN *at
his side. He turns to* STANDISH.)
BRADFORD: I count but five and forty adult males . . .
STANDISH: Five have remained below, sir . . . too ill to rise
from their pallets. (*Skeptically*) Or so they claim.
(BRADFORD *turns to the* SETTLERS.)
BRADFORD: My good people, we have summoned you together
to apprise you of our present situation, trusting that you
will view with forebearance and understanding the decision we are forced to make. (*There is a mutter of fore-
boding among the* SETTLERS *when* BRADFORD *pauses.*) We
will journey no further. With the help of God we will

establish ourselves on yonder shore. (*For a moment there is a shocked silence.*) And if God wills . . .

> (*Here he is interrupted by a swelling outburst of protest. Many of the voices are from those offstage, their voices overlapping; some from those in view.*)

SETTLERS: Nay! Nay! 'Tis madness! . . . Why? Why? Why here? . . . This is not Virginia! . . . We will have a say in this, sir! . . . We will not abide it, sir! . . . Treachery, Master Bradford, treachery!

BRADFORD (*over the voices*): Please! I beg of you, please! Hear me through!

> (*As the angry rumble subsides,* BILLINGTON's *voice carries over.*)

BILLINGTON (*demands*): Aye, give us answer, Master Bradford! Why here? We were bound for the Virginia plantations, were we not?

> (*The* SETTLERS *raise their voices again.*)

SETTLERS: Aye, give us answer, Master Bradford! . . . Why not on to Virginia? . . . Why this fearful land? (*Etc.*)

ALLERTON (*sharply*): If ye will just bear with Master Bradford he will give you answer! (*The hubbub subsides.*)

BREWSTER: Tell them, William. Tell these good people how, and why, we were forced to change our plans on the very day we sailed from Southampton.

BILLINGTON (*glowering, truculently*): 'Tis hard to credit that, Master Brewster.

FULLER: For shame, John Billington! How can you, or anyone, doubt the word of Elder Brewster? (*Some of the* SETTLERS *support* FULLER.)

SETTLERS: Aye, his word can be trusted . . . He's an honest God-fearing man . . . (*Etc.*)

BILLINGTON: Do ye take me for a simpleton? Only a bloody fool would believe . . .

ALDEN (*silencing him sharply*): Hold your clack, Billington!

> (BILLINGTON *swings around, makes a move toward* ALDEN, *but* TREVORE *steps between them.*)

TREVORE: Now, now, man . . .

BRADFORD (*sternly*): Billington! We can ill afford strife at

this moment! (BILLINGTON *glares at* ALDEN, *is met with
cold contempt. He turns away angrily.*) If you please,
Elder . . . the agreement from the London merchants.
(BREWSTER *takes a document from his pocket and hands
it to* BRADFORD. *He holds it up to the* SETTLERS.) This
. . . this is the contract the merchant-adventurers, who
financed our voyage, presented for our approval through
their agent Thomas Weston. They supplied the moneys
to charter this vessel, outfit it with food and goods to
carry us across the ocean, and see us through the long
winter to come. All at a rate of interest exorbitant beyond
all Christian conscience. Alas, we had no choice but to
accept. For we are all—all—poor people. And worldly
goods have we not. (*He extends his palms.*) All the
wealth we possess lies but in our stout hearts and the two
good hands the Lord bequeathed us. For humble working
men are we all. Farmers, artisans, laborers. Even as you,
John Alden, caskmaker. And you, Tom Tinker, wood
sawyer. (*Looking over their heads to offstage*) And you,
John Goodman, linen weaver. (*To* ALLERTON) Even as
you, Isaac Allerton, tailor. Or you, William Trevore,
mariner. Some among us have ventured forth to establish
a new church in this New World, where we may worship
in freedom, free from persecution. Others have come to
better their estate and build a better life for themselves
and their children. But, alas, to achieve this we agreed to
accept the cruel, harsh conditions demanded by the merchants. (*He looks at contract.*) Such as . . . to labor in
common, and place all our profits in trade, traffic, truck-
ing, working, fishing, or any other means . . . (*Looks up
in emphasis*) for seven years . . . seven long years . . .
FIRST SETTLER (*offstage, impatiently*): We know all that,
sir!
    (BRADFORD *holds up the contract, his hand trembling
    with indignation.*)
BRADFORD: Aye, but what ye don't know is that contained
in this contract, and inserted at the last moment, was a
demand that even after the moneys be paid back . . .

(*Stops*) fifty per cent of all our lands, homes and effects were to be retained to themselves and their heirs for all time to come!

(*After a moment of shocked silence, a rumble of angry indignation begins to swell.*)

SETTLERS: Those foul blood-suckers! . . . Filthy usurers! . . . Thieves! Bandits!

BRADFORD (*voice over tumult*): To slave for seven years without a day's freedom from task, and then to find . . .

MULLINS: 'Tis fit for thieves and bondslaves, not honest men!

HOPKINS (*accusingly*): And you agreed to abide by those outrageous terms?

BRADFORD: Nay, my friends, we refused to sign this contract . . . and that, on the very day we sailed from England.

SETTLERS: Well indeed! . . . You did well not to, sir! . . . We stand with you there! . . . May the Lord reward you!

BRADFORD (*gravely*): But, as a consequence, the syndicate washed its hands of the entire venture, refused to extend another penny to pay for the stores being withheld on the dock, unless we signed their unholy agreement. (*Over the angry growl from the* SETTLERS) And, by heaven, this we would not do!

SETTLERS: Aye, you did well not to! . . . A plague on those stone-hearted wretches! . . . God's curse on their greedy hands!

BRADFORD (*sadly*): Aye, we even had to sell some of our precious stores—our food and supplies—to pay the port duty before we could depart.

FLETCHER (*timidly*): Perhaps, Master Bradford, it might have been wiser to remain in port and come to some sort of compromise with the syndicate?

BRADFORD (*with a grim smile*): Compromise? As sure as God rules in heaven, they would have placed a lien on the vessel and all it contained. And that, Moses Fletcher, would have spelled the end of the venture, after all those long months of agony and labor.

SETTLERS: How true . . . Indeed, yes . . . They would have

done just that.

BRADFORD: And, what is more, many of us would have been cast into debtors' prison, there to rot for the rest of our miserable days. And how the bishops would have gloated at our fate! For, indeed, they hold no love for the Separatists. Nay, good friends, we had to get out, and get out fast. So we upped anchor and sailed with the tide. But what to do? Where to go? Virginia—without a charter? Nay, we would have suffered constant harassment. If not by the Crown, then by the bishops. And if not by the bishops, then by the syndicate, which has many a powerful friend at court. (*Pauses*) We had but one choice . . . to set a course for the Dutch domain on the Hudson River, where we could not be molested by the Crown, the bishops, or the London syndicate.

SETTLER (*offstage*): But, I pray you, Master Bradford, why then do we tarry here?

BRADFORD (*sighs*): Alas, 'twas the will of God that . . .

TREVORE (*breaks in*): The will of God . . . (*Looks at* JONES) or the will of Captain Jones, sir?

(JONES *moves up a step or two towards* TREVORE.)

JONES: Why, you scurvy wharf rat! I'll . . .

BREWSTER (*pleads*): Captain Jones, please! In God's name, let us have no violence!

TREVORE (*narrowly*): Tell me, Captain Jones, as one mariner to another—for I, too, have sailed many a year upon the seas—was it a mere navigational error upon your part to make landfall a full one hundred leagues north of your destination? (*As* JONES *glares at him*) Come, come, captain—an experienced mariner like you—'tis hard to credit, sir.

SETTLER (*offstage voice*): Aye, who bribed you, captain?

SECOND SETTLER: Who bribed you to keep us clear of the Dutch settlements, captain?

THIRD SETTLER (*offstage voice*): Was it Master Weston?

SETTLER (*offstage*): Show us your thirty pieces of silver, Captain Judas!

(JONES *places his hand on the butt of his pistol. The*

47

Bo'sn and two of the seamen move up closer to him.)

JONES: Who spoke there? Step forward and show your face, you lying, slanderous wretch! Come forward, if you dare! (BRADFORD jumps from hatch to head JONES off.)

BRADFORD: Captain Jones!

BILLINGTON (to JONES): By all that's holy, you'll order the anchor up and bear for the Hudson River or we'll take over the vessel and do so ourselves! Aye, friends?

THIRD SETTLER (offstage): Aye, let us do so, and be damned to him!

. (There is a closing of ranks among the SETTLERS as they press forward slowly toward JONES. JONES draws his pistol.)

JONES (orders): Bo'sn, pipe all hands!

(As the Bo'sn lifts the whistle that hangs from a thong around his neck, one of the settlers standing close by tears it away before he can bring it to his lips. The Bo'sn strikes him, sending him sprawling to the deck. By this time BRADFORD, STANDISH and some others step in between the two factions.)

BRADFORD: Get back! Stand back, all of ye! Billington! Dotey! Back!

JONES: You had better control them, sir! I'll have no mutiny on the Mayflower!

(The SETTLERS stand indecisively for a moment, then, as a mass, back up slowly.)

BRADFORD (demands): Put by your pistol, Captain Jones! (JONES hesitates, eyeing the SETTLERS apprehensively for a moment. Scowling, he tucks his pistol back into his belt.)

JONES: Very well! But I warn ye all . . . if anyone dare lay hand on any part of this vessel without order from me, I'll shoot him down for a mutineer! I . . . I and I alone am in sole command on this deck! And while ye remain aboard I am the law! Forget it at your peril!

BILLINGTON (with grim satisfaction): Aye, so be it. You are the law . . . while we remain aboard. (He turns to BRADFORD with insolent defiance.) But, once we leave this

vessel and step ashore . . . what then? Who then is the
law? The Crown? The Virginia Company? You? The
Elders? Nay, people, this is not Crown land! This is not
Company land! (*To* BRETHREN) Nor is it your land!
(*Turns back to* SETTLERS) I say, no one has authority
over us! (*As if just comprehending the situation, almost
afraid*) We are free! Free men! Free to do as we please!
And no mortal man has the right or the power to tell us
what to do!

(*Strangely enough, the* SETTLERS *seem to respond with
a feeling of uneasiness at the thought.*)

BRADFORD (*darkly, scathingly*): Free! Aye, free as a beast in
the jungle, Billington! And without the law of God to
guide you, or the law of man to contain you, you are no
more than a beast! And you will live and perish by the
law of the jungle . . . kill or be killed! (*He pauses to let
his words sink in, then turns to the* SETTLERS.) Is this
then what you wish?

(*There is a sober shaking of heads and a low murmur
of "nays."*)

BILLINGTON (*spitting on deck*): Pah! That's for the likes of
ye . . . ye craven, gutless bondslaves!

BRADFORD: And unless we create an authority, and a body of
law where none as yet exists, we will sink to the level of
the beast. So consider well the urgency of the moment,
and the need to strive together in close brotherhood, all
laboring for the common good. (*Pauses, stretches out his
hand to* BREWSTER) Elder . . . the compact. (BREWSTER
hands him the compact.) 'Twas with that thought in
mind, that the Elders have drawn up this compact . . . a
compact which ye are free to accept, or free to reject.
(*He enrolls it.*) Bear with me while I read it to you. (*He
reads.*) "In the name of God, Amen. We whose names are
underwritten, the loyal subjects of our dread sovereign
Lord, King James, by the grace of God, of Great Britain,
France, and Ireland, king defender of the faith, etc., having undertaken, for the glory of God, and advancement
of the Christian faith, and honor of our king and country,

a voyage to plant the first colony in the northern parts of Virginia, do by . . ." (*A comment is heard from* BILLINGTON *at this point, interrupting* BRADFORD *for a moment.*)

BILLINGTON: Virginia, indeed!

BRADFORD (*continues*): . . . "do by these present solemnly and mutually in the presence of God, and one of another, covenant and combine ourselves together into a civil body politic, for our better ordering and preservation and furtherance of the ends aforesaid; and by virtue hereof to enact, constitute and frame such just and equal laws, ordinances, acts, constitutions, and offices, from time to time, as shall be thought most meet and convenient for the general good of the colony, unto which we promise all due submission and obedience . . ." (*He is interrupted again by a scornful snort from* BILLINGTON.)

BILLINGTON: Hah! "submission and obedience," I pray thee!

BRADFORD (*after glancing up, continues*): "In witness whereof we have here-under subscribed our names at Cape Cod the 11th of November, in the year of the reign of our sovereign lord, King James of England, France, and Ireland the eighteenth, and of Scotland the fifty-fourth. Anno Domino 1620."

(*When* BRADFORD *finishes reading, he drops his arms and gazes in silence at the* SETTLERS, *wondering how they have received it. There's a mutter and a murmur of low conversation among them. Some look deeply puzzled, not having quite grasped the full significance of the compact. Others look thoughtful.* BRADFORD *lifts the document into reading position again.*)

BRADFORD: Subscribing unto this covenant, and signing there-under, are: John Carver, William Bradford, Edward Winslow, William Brewster, Isaac Allerton, Miles Standish, Deacon Fuller and Christopher Martin. (*He lowers the compact.*) We urge you all to lend your names and support to this compact. And it matters not if your station be master, goodman, hired man or servant.

TINKER: Master Bradford . . .

BRADFORD: Aye, Tom Tinker?

TINKER: Indeed, 'twould be a great kindness, your worship, if you explained in simple wordings the meaning therein. Read nor write can I, and my poor unlettered mind got entangled in the brambles of all those aforesaids, here-to-fores, where-as-es and . . . and such like.

BRADFORD (*sincerely*): We beg your forgiveness, Thomas. In simple terms, good people, by this compact we bind ourselves into a body politic to elect officers who will frame just and equal laws for the common good of all.

TINKER (*doubtfully*): Hmm . . . 'tis a goodly thought, Master Bradford . . . but how can there be a law for the common good of all? For, of a certainty, what is good for the master, cannot be good for the servant. Aye, such has always been the order of things, and, I fear me, 'twill always be so.

BRADFORD: But, Thomas, under a government elected by the people—all the people—a government granting the same rights and liberties to rich and poor, master and servant alike, favoring neither one nor the other, holding all equal in the sight of God and man, granting freedom . . .

BILLINGTON: Words! Mere words! And I trust them not . . . (*Pointing to compact.*) Whether they be writ on parchment or fall from the lips of mortal man! And I'll thank ye not to grant me my freedom, when freedom is mine to be had the hour I set foot on that shore where neither king nor clergy rule! Nay, I, for one, will sign no document that binds me to the will of anyone, be it a man, or be it a government!

(BRADFORD *looks at* BILLINGTON *sadly. He lifts his eyes to the* SETTLERS.)

BRADFORD: If any one is of like mind, let him speak now.

FIRST SETTLER (*offstage*): I will not sign!

SECOND SETTLER (*offstage*): Nor will I!

MULLINS (*turning toward voice defiantly*): I, William Mullins of Dorking, Surrey, will sign!

ALDEN: And I, John Alden, cooper of Harwich, Essex, will sign.

TREVORE: Without a firm hand at the helm, and a star to

steer by, a ship will founder. I, William Trevore, mariner . . . (*Smiles*) from neither here nor there, but everywhere, will sign . . . (*Lower*) to find me a home from the sea.

BROWNE (*shaking his head*): 'Tis but a dream. A wondrous dream . . . but a dream withall . . .

DOTEY (*hesitantly, as he casts a timid glance at* HOPKINS): Your worship . . .

BRADFORD: Aye, Edward Dotey?

DOTEY: I am but a lowly indenture . . . servant to Master Hopkins. (*Looks at* LEISTER) As is Edward Leister here. Liberty is not for the likes of us for seven years hence. As it is not for the eighteen souls who are indentured as I. (*Stops to look at* HOPKINS *again*) Now, sir, if the likes of us chose not to sign . . .

HOPKINS (*breaking in, outraged*): What! Why you impudent scoundrel! You'll sign! Both of you! You are bound by law to serve me for seven years! And, by God, you'll obey my every wish, or I'll . . .

BILLINGTON (*derisively*): Or you'll fetch them up before the court in Old Bailey in London Town, aye, Master Hopkins?

HOPKINS: They are bound by the law . . . the law of the land . . .

SECOND SETTLER (*offstage, with a laugh*): What law? What land, Master Hopkins?

(HOPKINS *turns an angry, frustrated look at* BRADFORD.)

HOPKINS: They'll sign! I'll make them sign!

BRADFORD: Nay, sir. No one can, or will be forced to sign this covenant against his will. I'd rather have it cast into the sea and have done with it, than see us raise the structure of our society on a cornerstone of tyranny, Master Hopkins.

HOPKINS: But they are indentures . . . articled to me . . . their master!

BRADFORD: We are all indentured servants to the one and only Master, sir! The Lord God in heaven Himself! And He shall be the sole master to whom we will bow our heads or bend our knee! (*He pauses, changes his tone,*

appeals.) Brothers all . . . before God, let us pledge ourselves to strive together in a spirit of love and brotherhood, to build a commonwealth founded on the will of
all men. A free society the like of which the world has
not seen . . . (*With a smile at* BROWNE) or dreamed of
. . . where one may worship in full freedom of conscience,
and glorify His name with renewed faith . . . in a new
world.

> (*There is a hush for a while, then* LEISTER *speaks up
> quietly.*)

LEISTER: I will sign.

DOTEY (*nods*): And I . . . (*Looks at* HOPKINS *with pride
and spirit*) I, Edward Dotey, of the London gutter, will
sign. (*With emphasis.*) But of my own free will, mark ye!

> (*Solemn affirmations come from many more of the
> SETTLERS.*)

SETTLERS: And I . . . And so will I . . . And I.

CARVER (*low, fervently*): His will be done . . . Let us give
thanks to the Lord for bringing us safely across the sea.
Let us praise the Lord, for His mercies endureth forever.
And though we may wander in the wilderness as the children of Israel, at times hungry and thirsty, let us maintain
faith in His goodness and divine guidance through all the
trials of the flesh and the spirit . . . that is ours to come.

> (*The* SETTLERS *bow their heads and begin kneeling on
> the deck.* JONES *is seen to hesitate. His eyes are lowered,
> and he is biting his lip. Then he kneels down, casting
> a glance at the* Bo'SN, *who quickly follows suit. The
> SEAMEN look at the captain in open-mouthed surprise,
> but the* Bo'SN *turns a lowering glance in their direc-
> tion and they quickly get to their knees when they see
> him running his fingers through the strands of the
> cat-o'-nine-tails. We hear them all intoning the Lord's
> prayer, as the curtain begins to descend.*)

ALL: Our Father, who art in heaven, Hallowed be thy Name.
Thy kingdom come. Thy will be done, on earth as it is in
heaven. Give us this day our daily bread. And forgive us
our debts, as we forgive our debtors. And lead us not into

temptation, but deliver us from evil. For thine is the kingdom, and the power, and the glory, for ever. Amen.

CURTAIN

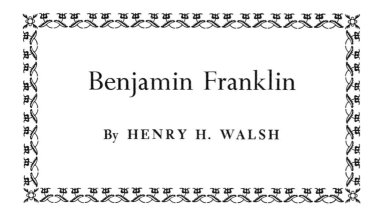

Benjamin Franklin

By HENRY H. WALSH

BENJAMIN FRANKLIN

CHARACTERS: 8 males; 2 females
(There are 7 additional male
characters and groups of offstage voices
that can be doubled at will in casting)

PLAYING TIME: 60 minutes

SET: One double—varied with
properties.

✍ Historical Notes

BENJAMIN FRANKLIN once remarked to his wife, "Debby, I wish the good Lord had made each day twice as long as it is, then I could really accomplish something." So spoke Benjamin Franklin, printer, author, publisher, inventor, businessman, scientist, philosopher, statesman, diplomat, and, above all, humanist.

He was born in Boston, Massachusetts, on January 17, 1706, the fifteenth in a family of seventeen children. When he was eight years old, his father, a candlemaker by trade, sent him to school after Benjamin had learned to read and write by himself. But Josiah Franklin, being too poor to spend money on education for his huge family, was forced to withdraw Benjamin from school and put him to work in his candlemaking shop. And that two years of schooling was the extent of Franklin's formal education.

When he was apprenticed to his brother James in his printing shop at the age of twelve, he gave up eating meat and became a vegetarian, not because of principle, but to save money to buy books, a very scarce and expensive item in those days. Perhaps it was the memory of those days that induced him to establish the first free circulating public library in Pennsylvania in the year 1730. Shortly thereafter, he formed the first fire department in Philadelphia; helped establish the first American fire-insurance company; reformed the police system; organized the first public hospital in America (the Pennsylvania Hospital); and planned and founded the Academy of Pennsylvania, which is now the

University of Pennsylvania.

As a scientist, being a very practical man, he was not content with just saying, "An ounce of prevention is worth a pound of cure." He backed it up with the invention of (among numerous other things) the lightning rod, in his effort to prove that lightning and electricity were one and the same thing, thus saving countless lives and uncounted costs in the destruction of property. It may have been his avid interest in scientific research which compelled him to teach himself how to read books written in French, Latin, Italian, Spanish, and German.

A tabulation and description of his inventions, innovations, and scientific experiments would fill a book, as would his contributions to the welfare and advancement of America in his capacity of statesman and politician.

But what marks the true genius of Benjamin Franklin?

When, at the age of forty-two, he was wealthy enough to retire from business (feeling, as he said, that "A wise man will desire no more than what he may get justly, use soberly, distribute cheerfully, and leave contentedly"), he indicated what may have been the very core and spirit of the man, the capacity to live life fully, and, at the same time, to give of himself unstintingly to his friends, to his community, to his country, and to the world.

✏ Production Notes

⟦ Characters

NOTE: Benjamin Franklin is presented in three separate roles in the play: BEN, BENJAMIN and FRANKLIN.

BEN, *Benjamin Franklin at the age of 84*
MIRROR, *a voice*
JAMES FRANKLIN, *Benjamin Franklin's older brother*
BENJAMIN, *Benjamin Franklin at the age of 15*
FRANKLIN, *Benjamin Franklin at the age of 42 to 70*
DEBORAH FRANKLIN, *Benjamin Franklin's wife*
FIRST JUNTO MEMBER
SECOND JUNTO MEMBER
THIRD JUNTO MEMBER
FOURTH JUNTO MEMBER
FIRST ASSEMBLYMAN, *an offstage voice*
ASSEMBLYMEN, *offstage voices*
PEOPLE, *the offstage voices of a moving crowd*
SPEAKER, *of the House of Commons*
SCRIBE, *of the House of Commons*
FIRST MEMBER, *of the House of Commons, an offstage voice*
SECOND MEMBER, *of the House of Commons, an offstage voice*
THIRD MEMBER, *of the House of Commons, an offstage voice*
FOURTH MEMBER, *of the House of Commons, an offstage voice*
SALLY, *Benjamin Franklin's daughter*
THOMAS JEFFERSON, *author of the Declaration of Independence*
THOMAS PAINE, *political writer*
FIVE PATRIOTS, *American soldiers*
GENERAL GEORGE WASHINGTON

⟦ Scenes

Scene 1: Ben's study in Philadelphia, 1790.
Scene 2: James Franklin's printing shop in Boston, 1722.

Scene 3: Street in Philadelphia, 1723.

Scene 4: Ben's workshop in Philadelphia, 1748.

Scene 5: Meeting room of the Junto in a private residence.

Scene 6: The rostrum in the Pennsylvania Assembly Chamber, 1757.

Scene 7: The rostrum in the House of Commons, London, 1766.

Scene 8: Ben's workshop in Philadelphia, 1775.

Scene 9: The Speaker's platform in Independence Hall, 1776.

Scene 10: Campfire at Valley Forge, winter, 1777.

THE 10 SCENES in the play may be presented simply and impressionistically with a minimum of properties and staging. For clarity, Benjamin Franklin is characterized in the play as BEN, BENJAMIN and FRANKKLIN as he progresses in age. A double for old BEN is required in Scenes 4, 5, 6, 7, and 8. The play is presented on a divided stage. Stage section right remains the same throughout the play, with lights dimming down as stage section left is exposed behind gauze and amber light.

SCENE 1

([Costumes

Ben wears the clothing of the period, but his clothing is almost entirely covered by the long dressing-robe he wears throughout the play on stage section right. On his feet are comfortable slippers.

([Properties

Bookcase and books; desk; inkpot and quill pen; 2 candlesticks and candles; dressing-table with a tall mirror; semi-upholstered high-backed chair; cane; pair of square-cut spectacles; rug.

([Lighting

The effect of candlelight, dimming down as action goes to stage section right.

SCENE 2

([**Costumes**

Benjamin is dressed in the shirt, knee breeches, stockings and shoes of the period. His shirt-sleeves are rolled up and he wears a long, ink-stained apron over his clothing. James is dressed in the same manner.

([**Properties**

A long work table; a pile of single sheet (tabloid size) newspapers; a letter size paper, folded in three and sealed; a pica rule.

([**Lighting**

Scene is played behind gauze, with daylight entering from left.

SCENE 3

([**Costumes**

Benjamin is dressed as in Scene 2, but without the apron. In addition he wears a cocked hat, vest and coat of the period. The sleeve of a spare shirt dangles from his coat pocket and a pair of stockings from the other.

([**Properties**

Two long loaves of bread.

([**Setting**

A backdrop showing the fronts and steps of several attached colonial houses.

([**Lighting**

Daylight diffused.

SCENE 4

([**Costumes**

Franklin is wearing the clothing of the period. He wears no

coat but has a vest. The same long ink-stained apron covers his clothing. Deborah wears a long colonial house gown, covered by an equally long white apron tied around the waist. On her head she wears the white hood worn by women in those days.

⟪ Properties

A long work bench, cluttered with strange gadgets and contrivances: bell jars; wires, etc. A couple of chairs before the table.

⟪ Lighting

Daylight entering from left.

SCENE 5

⟪Costumes

Franklin and the four other Junto members are fully dressed in the clothing of the period. Their vests and coats are quite colorful, indicating their status as gentlemen in the community. They wear no wigs, have their hair tied back with colorful velvet ribbons.

⟪ Properties

A long tavern table; five pewter tankards; a wicker-covered jug; five chairs; several prints on the back wall.

⟪ Lighting

Daylight enters through two floor-length windows in back wall.

SCENE 6

⟪ Costumes

Franklin, the chairman and the two other Assembly members wear white formal wigs.

⟪ **Properties**

A stepped-up platform; three straight-backed semi-upholstered chairs; a table before the chairman.

⟪ **Lighting**

Diffused daylight.

SCENE 7

⟪ **Costumes**

Franklin wears a white wig. The Speaker wears the long
elaborate wig that is traditionally worn by members of
Parliament. The scribe, a simple white wig.

⟪ **Properties**

A high, step-up platform for the Speaker of the House.
His chair is a very elaborate affair, very much like a throne.
The scribe is seated at a small table; before him, an
inkpot, quills and several sheets of foolscap.

⟪ **Lighting**

Directed beams of daylight, streaming in from left and right,
as if coming from several windows unseen.

SCENE 8

⟪ **Costumes**

Franklin is dressed as before, but wears a different coat. He
wears no wig. Sally is dressed in the same manner as
Deborah in Scene 4.

⟪ **Properties**

The same as in Scene 4.

⟪ **Lighting**

Daylight entering from left.

SCENE 9

❲ Costumes

Jefferson is dressed in simple, dark clothing of the period. He wears no wig; his hair is tied by a dark ribbon behind him.

❲ Properties

No properties or setting.

❲ Lighting

An amber spot is on Jefferson as he reads.

SCENE 10

❲ Costumes

The five patriots wear the uniform of the Continental army, considerably tattered and soiled. They wear greatcoats over their uniforms. Scarves are bound over their heads and tied around their throats. Their feet are covered in wrapped gunnysacking. Cocked hats are worn over their scarf-covered heads. Paine is in the uniform of the Continentals. He is hatless. Washington wears a greatcoat over his uniform. A sword hangs from his side.

❲ Properties

Five muskets; small sticks of wood for the campfire; a red electric light under the logs to simulate a fire; a drum; a sheet of paper; inkpot and quill pen.

❲ Lighting

The fading light of late afternoon in winter.

"Benjamin Franklin"

Scene I

Scene II

65

Benjamin Franklin

SCENE 1

A divided stage. On stage right, BEN's study; the other half, stage left, remains in darkness behind gauze curtain until the action performed on stage left requires light and exposure, behind gauze. BEN's study contains a book-filled bookcase set against the back wall, a desk standing close by with an inkpot, quill pen, and two lighted candlesticks. Left front, a dressing table with a tall mirror mounted upon it. The mirror is slightly turned away from the audience to avoid any reflection upon its surface. The dressing table and mirror stand away from the wall to provide space for a concealed performer who is the voice of the MIRROR. A comfortable chair faces the mirror.

At curtain rise BEN, old and feeble, shuffles in from right, supporting himself with a cane. He walks to the desk, picks up a candle and searches for a book, peering over his square-cut spectacles. He selects a book, tucks it under his arm and, candle in hand, walks to the dressing table. As he places the book and candle down on the table, he glances casually into the mirror. Evidently he doesn't like what he sees, for he frowns, leans forward to regard himself more critically. He shakes his head with a rueful smile.

66

BEN: La, but you are a sad, sad sight, Benjamin Franklin. (*As he starts to walk away the* MIRROR *speaks.*)

MIRROR (*gravely*): Indeed you be, Ben.

BEN (*as if he always suspected it*): Oh, so mirrors can talk. (*With a sniff of distaste*) But, I pray you, where did you come by that horrible voice?

MIRROR (*demands*): And what is wrong with my voice?

BEN: Sounds like a voice from the grave. (*Shortly*) And I like it not.

MIRROR (*offended*): Indeed! Humm . . . Nonetheless, I don't sound as bad as you *look*, Ben Franklin.

BEN: Never you mind my looks! (*He sits down and regards the mirror critically for a moment.*) You don't look much better yourself, I must say.

MIRROR (*thoughtfully*): 'S'truth . . . 's'truth, I don't. (*Brightens*) Ah, but my future prospects are far better than yours, my friend.

BEN (*pleads*): I pray you, let us not reflect on my future. In truth, I'd much prefer you reflected on my past.

MIRROR: Well, now, that's a thought. And I do feel in a reflective mood this evening at that.

BEN: Ah, good, good. (*Tentatively*) Then, could you . . . would you take me back a bit . . . into the past?

MIRROR: How far would you like me to go, Ben?

BEN (*decisively*): The farther the better. Aye, the farther— (BEN *stops short at the loud wail of a baby.*) Heavens above! Nay, nay, let us not go through *that* again! Please!

MIRROR (*crossly*): But you said . . . Oh, very well, very well. (*Wail stops abruptly.* BEN *emits an audible sigh of relief.*) But where would you have me start?

BEN (*reflectively*): Mmm . . . when I was fifteen. Yes, fifteen. That will do . . .

MIRROR (*trying to recall*): Hmmm . . . fifteen . . . fifteen. . . .

SCENE 2

The light begins to dim stage right, until just candlelight remains. Simultaneously, lights stage left go slowly up behind

the gauze drop, revealing the interior of a printing shop.
BENJAMIN, *aged fifteen, is counting out folio-sized papers at
a table.*

BEN (*as if seeing it in the mirror*): Aye, my brother James'
   print shop in Boston Town . . . Queen Street . . . where
   I was apprenticed. . . .
BENJAMIN (*counting*): . . . Forty-five . . . forty-six . . . forty-
   seven . . . forty-eight . . . forty-nine . . . (*Emphatically*)
   Fifty! (*Calls out*) Five hundred and fifty, brother James!
      (JAMES *appears. He holds a long pica rule in one hand
      and a paper in the other.*)
JAMES: That should do, Benjamin. Break type and begin com-
   posing the reverse page. (*Hands* BENJAMIN *the paper*) And
   make space for this advertisement from Widow Hawkins.
      (BENJAMIN *reads the advertisement to himself. A broad
      grin forms on his face.*)
BENJAMIN (*chuckling*): This advertisement, brother James . . .
JAMES (*scowling*): Seems to strike you funny. And what is
   so humorous about it?
BENJAMIN (*controlling laughter*): Could bear a mite of correction methinks—
JAMES: Correction? (*He snatches paper from* BENJAMIN *and
   reads it over to himself, then looks up with a scowl.*) I see
   naught amiss with this. (*Reads it aloud*) "To be sold by
   Widow Hawkins—one Holstein cow, warranted to give at
   each milking, ten quarts of milk and a pair of handsome
   bronze andirons."
      (JAMES *glares at* BENJAMIN, *who cannot control his
      giggles.*)
BENJAMIN (*trying hard to control his expression*): Does it
   not appear to you a most amazing creature, brother James?
JAMES (*blankly*): Amazing? (*Very cross*) You get on with
   your work and leave the writing to me!
BENJAMIN (*as if just remembering, innocently*): Oh, by the
   by . . . another one of those mysterious notes was slipped
   under the door while you were out.
      (BENJAMIN *begins to search through his pockets, de-*

liberately teasing JAMES, pretending he can't find the note.)

JAMES (eagerly): From Mistress Dogood?

BENJAMIN: Aye. (Murmurs) Now, where could I have . . . I'm certain I put it in one of my pockets . . .

JAMES (lifting his stick): You little addlepate! If you've lost it I'll . . .

(BENJAMIN backs away, then takes the note from his pocket.)

BENJAMIN: Ah, here it be!

(JAMES snatches it from his hand, breaks the seal and eagerly begins to read it. He begins to chuckle. BENJAMIN watches him with a sly smile on his face.)

JAMES: Oh, this is good! This is famous! 'Tis no wonder the whole town of Boston is talking about her comments in our paper!

BENJAMIN: Now, I wonder who she could be?

JAMES: Ha, whoever she be, she of a certainty whittles a sharp quill!

BENJAMIN: What does she write this time, James?

JAMES (dismissing him): You just go about your work. Your puny little brain won't comprehend the subtle barbs of this witty old dame anyway.

BENJAMIN (sniffs): Indeed!

JAMES: We must publish another appeal, asking her to reveal her identity.

BENJAMIN (in a huff): That won't be at all necessary, dear brother. I know where she can be spoke with at any time twixt the hours of seven and seven.

JAMES: What? You do . . . ?

BENJAMIN: Aye, right here, at the printing shop of James Franklin in Queen Street!

JAMES: What manner of nonsense . . .

BENJAMIN: No nonsense at all! (Points to floor) Mistress Silence Dogood is right here in this shop (Taps his apron) behind this apron!

JAMES (with a scornful laugh): Do you expect me to believe . . . ?

BENJAMIN: The note came sealed, did it not?

JAMES (*his eyes narrow*): It did.

BENJAMIN (*quoting from memory*): "Dear Sirs and Gentle Readers, (JAMES *is checking the note, his face tightening with anger and surprise.*) If a certain gentleman, Mr. B. were to spend more of his leisure . . . (JAMES *begins to advance on* BENJAMIN *with his stick raised to strike.* BENJAMIN *backs away.*) . . . time . . . (BENJAMIN *dodges behind the table.* JAMES *circles around, trying to get at him with the stick.*)

JAMES (*furious*): Why, you impudent whelp!

BENJAMIN: Now, now, brother James, put by your stick!

JAMES (*stalking him*): So, you are Mistress Dogood, are you? Well, by heavens, I'll do you good with this stick, I will! (*He whacks* BENJAMIN.)

BENJAMIN: Owww . . . Don't, brother! (BENJAMIN *circles around the table with* JAMES *following, swinging his stick.*)

JAMES: Neglect your work, will you! Steal my time with your confounded scribbling, will you! I'll teach you, *Mistress Dogood!*

(BENJAMIN *manages to get to the exit.*)

BENJAMIN (*rubbing his shoulder*): Aye, yes indeed, that beastly stick of yours has been a most ardent teacher! It has shortened my apprenticeship with you by many a year!

JAMES: And what do you mean by that?

BENJAMIN: I'm bidding you fare-thee-well! I'm leaving you and your blasted print shop, and your beastly stick! (*Exiting*) So, farewell, brother James! (*Offstage*) Farewell to you!

(JAMES *follows him to the exit.*)

JAMES (*calling out*): Don't you dare! Don't you dare run off! If you do, I'll see to it that you never get employment again in Boston! (*As the lights begin to fade down, stage left.*) And you had better bear that in mind, Benjamin Franklin! (*As the lights dim down slowly to black, stage left, the lights, stage right, up gradually.* BEN *is seated as before, lost in his memories of the past.*)

MIRROR: But you did, Ben, didn't you? (BEN *doesn't answer.*

SCENE 3

He appears to have dozed off, but he hasn't.) Ben . . . ?
BEN *(lifting his head with a start)*: Eh?
MIRROR: I thought you had dozed off.
BEN *(rubbing his forehead)*: Nooo, just wool gathering, I guess . . . What were you saying?
MIRROR: I said you did.
BEN: Did *what?*
MIRROR: Run away from Boston and your brother James.
BEN *(vaguely)*: Did I?
MIRROR: Don't you remember?
BEN: It . . . it was so long ago . . . so long ago . . .
MIRROR: You ran off to New York. But you couldn't find ready employment there as a printer. So you journeyed on to Philadelphia. Remember now?

SCENE 3

During the above the lights, stage left, go up slowly behind gauze, revealing BENJAMIN. *He stands holding a long loaf of bread under each arm, munching a chunk he has broken off, looking about him with a grin of avid interest in what he sees.*

BEN *(with a chuckle)*: Ah, yes, yes, I remember.
MIRROR *(chuckling)*: Oh, but you were a sight to behold when you set foot in Philadelphia. Dirty . . . tired . . . your pockets stuffed with shirts and socks . . . with a sleeve dangling fore, and a shirt streaming aft. *(Chuckle)* Yes, indeed, a sight to behold.
BEN *(with a wide grin)*: And with naught but a Dutch dollar in my pocket. *(As* BENJAMIN *wanders off to exit, stage left goes to black.)* Keimer . . . old Keimer the printer gave me employment. I worked hard at the printing trade. *(Pointedly)* And I saved my money. Twenty-one I was when I left Keimer and opened my own shop. Prospered, didn't I? Published my own newspaper.
MIRROR: And the Almanac, Ben.
BEN: Aye, the Almanac. *(Still a wonder to him)* Ten thou-

71

sand copies a year it sold. Ten thousand . . . and it brought me wealth.

MIRROR: And renown . . . renown. I warrant you were the most widely quoted writer in the colonies. Poor Richard's sayings were on everyone's tongue. (*Quotes*) "Early to bed, and early to rise, makes a man healthy, wealthy and wise." Ha! Never saw you bedded down before midnight, Ben.

BEN (*murmurs*): 'Tis best to do as the preacher says . . . not as he does.

MIRROR (*continues quoting, as if he is about to go on endlessly*): "A penny saved is a penny earned." . . . "He who goes a-borrowing goes a-sorrowing." . . . "Keep your—"

BEN (*interrupts, shortly, with a lifted palm*): 'Twill do! 'Twill do!

MIRROR: I was only about to quote Poor Richard on the subject of marriage.

BEN: Marriage?

MIRROR: Aye. (*Quotes*) "Keep your eyes wide open before marriage, and half shut afterwards." (*Chuckles*) Did you follow that precept yourself when you took to wife Deborah Reid, Ben?

BEN (*fondly*): Ah, Debby. A good wife . . . a good wife. My dear practical Debby.

MIRROR (*judgmental*): Aye, she was that, if anything . . . practical.

SCENE 4

During above, the lights, stage left, go gradually up, revealing FRANKLIN, *age 42, tinkering with some wires and gadgets in his workshop. His bench is cluttered with strange contrivances and jars. He is so absorbed, he is not aware of* DEBORAH's *entrance. She is looking at* FRANKLIN, *shaking her head in disapproval.*

DEBORAH: Ben (*He doesn't hear her so she calls louder.*) Benjamin!

FRANKLIN (*startled, turns around*): Oh, Debby, my dear. I

didn't hear you come in. (*He turns back to his tinkering.*)

DEBORAH (*annoyed*): Don't you get weary just staying to home, tinkering with those silly wires? (FRANKLIN *is so absorbed he doesn't answer.*) Benjamin, you are not even listening!

FRANKLIN (*turns, with a start*): Eh, what? Forgive me, Debby. What were you saying, my love?

DEBORAH (*with a weary sigh*): It matters not. I just asked— (*She stops, as bells tinkle in the distance.*) Do I hear bells, Benjamin? Or do my ears . . . ?

FRANKLIN (*with a delighted chuckle*): You do indeed, my dear.

DEBORAH: Who could be ringing bells? Where does it come from?

FRANKLIN: From the attic.

DEBORAH: The attic?

FRANKLIN: You see, I have wires strung from my lightning rod to some bells. When a thunderstorm is brewing, the bells ring.

DEBORAH (*sniffs*): That lightning rod! Another one of your silly experiments!

FRANKLIN: I'll have you know, that lightning rod is no more an experiment. Why, do you know that the King of France had some placed on the roof of his palace? (*Chuckles*) They say that the Tuilleries looks like the back of a porcupine with his dander up.

DEBORAH: Parson Pearson said last Sunday that your lightning rod was nothing more than flying in the face of Providence.

FRANKLIN: He would do better to place one a-top his steeple.

DEBORAH: And, furthermore, it's shameful . . . a man of your age, forty-two . . .

FRANKLIN (*thoughtfully*): Forty-two . . . hmmm.

DEBORAH: Aye, forty-two, the father of two children, chasing through the pastures and flying a kite like a witless lad! (FRANKLIN *is not listening, he is thinking.*)

FRANKLIN: Forty-two. (*Decisively*) You know, Debby, I think I'll retire.

DEBORAH (*shocked*): Retire?

FRANKLIN: Aye, sell my printing shop, newspaper . . . everything. Retire.

DEBORAH: At your age? What in the name of goodness has gotten into you?

FRANKLIN: Debby, I've worked hard all my life, and I've accumulated enough wealth to take care of all our needs. So, I'll spend the rest of my life reading the books I love, and engaging in scientific experiments.

DEBORAH: I think you should be ashamed, aye, downright ashamed to retire to a life of leisure at your age!

FRANKLIN: There's nothing shameful in a wish to enjoy leisure.

DEBORAH: But, heavenly saints, the best years of your life are ahead of you!

FRANKLIN: Truly so, and I don't intend wasting those precious years in the vain pursuit of more money. We have enough. And more than enough is too much.

DEBORAH: Who ever heard of *too* much money!

FRANKLIN: Ah, Debby my dear, when one has too much money, he does not possess wealth, it possesses him. In truth, my love, wealth is not his that has it, but his that enjoys it. I'm going to be one that enjoys it. (*Thunder sounds offstage as* FRANKLIN's *bells tinkle louder.* FRANKLIN, *with almost childish delight, starts to rush off.*) See, Debby! Here comes my storm!

DEBORAH (*scolds*): Benjamin, you're not going to . . . ?

FRANKLIN (*as he exits*): Aye, I'm off to the pasture to fly my kite!

(DEBORAH *stands looking in the direction of his exit, shakes her head with a hopeless sigh, as the lights dim down and go to black on stage left. Action goes back to stage right.*)

MIRROR: Remember how absorbed you were in your experiments, Ben? How people flocked to your house to see the wondrous things you wrought? Aye, even England and France began hearing of Benjamin Franklin.

BEN: Ah, yes, they published my paper, proving that electricity and lightning were of the same nature.

MIRROR (*chuckles*): And just by flying a kite.

BEN (*sighs, longingly*): Ah, but those were good days, good days. Life was so full, so pleasant . . . My books . . . my experiments.

MIRROR: And the Junto, Ben.

BEN (*vaguely*): Junto? . . . Junto?

SCENE 5

The lights, stage left, go up slowly, revealing FRANKLIN *and four other* JUNTO MEMBERS *seated around a long table.*

MIRROR: The club you formed in Philadelphia.

BEN (*nods*): I recall now. We used to meet regularly . . . every Friday evening . . .

FIRST MEMBER: Tonight, fellow members of the Junto, Ben has a new plan he wishes to present for our consideration . . .

SECOND MEMBER: Which, he no doubt will claim, as usual, some folks suggested to him. (*The* MEMBERS *laugh.*)

THIRD MEMBER: Tell us, Ben . . . what folks?

FRANKLIN (*growls*): I'm not the only mortal in Philadelphia with ideas.

FOURTH MEMBER: Perhaps not. But who thought of the first free public library in America?

FIRST MEMBER: And the first organized fire department . . .

SECOND MEMBER: Street cleaning department . . .

THIRD MEMBER: Police department.

FRANKLIN (*hastily*): Well, be that as it may; nevertheless, I chanced to speak with—

MEMBERS (*interrupting, in unison*): Some folks!
    (*Laughter;* FRANKLIN *joins in.*)

FRANKLIN: On my honor, friends, this time it is true. The proposal I am about to make was suggested to me by Doctor Thomas Bond. And I'm sure it has been thought of by many, for the need should be evident to all.

FIRST MEMBER: What are you referring to, Ben?

FRANKLIN: It concerns the sick: the needy souls who have

been streaming into the city of late from the surrounding countryside—

FOURTH MEMBER (*growling*): Aye, and carrying heaven knows what contagions!

THIRD MEMBER (*soberly*): They do create a problem indeed. There is no place for them to stay.

FRANKLIN: And none care, or dare to take them in.

SECOND MEMBER: Can't blame folks, Ben. A man has to protect his own.

FRANKLIN: That all may be very true, but we can't see people perish in the streets of Philadelphia for lack of care.

FIRST MEMBER: What do you propose, Ben?

FRANKLIN: I propose we discuss ways and means to establish a refuge for the sick and needy; an institution staffed with competent physicians and nurses.

THIRD MEMBER (*doubtfully*): A public hospital?

FRANKLIN: Yes, a free public hospital . . . just that.

MEMBERS (*doubtfully murmur*): A free hospital? That will take money . . . Aye, a great sum of money.

FIRST MEMBER: Where will it come from, Ben?

FRANKLIN: I was thinking . . . we might raise the funds through popular subscription. (*As the* MEMBERS *look thoughtfully at each other.*) Just think of it, gentlemen. Philadelphia will have the great honor of establishing the first free hospital in America.

(*The lights, stage left, fade to black as action goes back to stage right.*)

MIRROR: Those years were indeed very interesting, pleasant and fruitful, Ben.

BEN (*regretfully*): Ah, but it didn't last very long, did it?

MIRROR (*accusingly*): Nay, you had to go and get yourself elected a member of the Pennsylvania Assembly . . . and walk into a mess of trouble!

BEN (*defensively*): It was nothing *I* willed!

MIRROR: So I've heard you claim before. My, my, those were stormy days in the Assembly.

BEN (*trying to recall*): Aye, there was great rancor among the assemblymen. (*Hazily*) I . . . I recall not the matter.

It . . . it was so long ago . . .

MIRROR (*quietly*): Taxes, Ben . . . taxes. It was about taxes, remember?

BEN: Ah, yes . . . taxes. (*A random association*) There are only two sure things in life, death and taxes. (*Chuckles*) How clever! (*Begins to repeat*) There are—(*Stops, admiringly*) Now, I wonder who said that?

MIRROR: You did, Ben. A long time ago.

BEN (*pleased*): Did I indeed? (*Remembers*) I recall now what the fuss was about. It concerned the Penn family, and the other wealthy proprietors who controlled huge estates and revenues, yet paid not a penny of taxes to the treasury.

MIRROR: Which prompted you to make quite a speech in the Pennsylvania Assembly, quite a speech.

SCENE 6

The lights, stage left, go up. FRANKLIN *is standing, facing the Assembly, who are offstage and unseen by the audience. Behind* FRANKLIN, *seated on a raised platform, are the* CHAIRMAN *of the Assembly and two* ASSEMBLY MEMBERS.

FRANKLIN (*projecting*): Whether or no the mother country has the right to place such a huge burden upon the people of Pennsylvania is not the question at this moment!

FIRST ASSEMBLYMAN (*voice offstage*): Then what *is* the question, if not just that, Mr. Franklin?

FRANKLIN: We need to be concerned only with *this* matter: Is it just for the wealthiest among us to go scot free of taxes while the poorer and—yes, the more industrious—bear the heavy obligations placed upon us by the Crown?

ASSEMBLYMEN (*voices offstage*): Nay, it is not just! The Penn family must bear an equal share of the taxes! The Governor is favoring them! This must not be!

FIRST ASSEMBLYMAN: But they have the power of the Crown behind them, Mr. Franklin! There is nothing we can do about it!

77

FRANKLIN: We must do something about it, gentlemen. We can't afford to stand by and see a disposition among the wealthy to establish in this colony an aristocracy of privilege in government!

(*There are applause and cries of agreement.*)

ASSEMBLYMEN: Hear! Hear! . . . This must not be! . . . It is unjust!

FRANKLIN: Nay, it is not justice, gentlemen. And if His Excellency, the Governor of Pennsylvania, will not bear with us on this issue, then it behooves us to take our cause to the Court of St. James and present it to the king!

(*More applause and cries of approval, as stage left goes black and action returns to stage right.*)

MIRROR (*marveling*): And a very, very pretty speech that was, Ben.

BEN (*grumbles*): I should have kept my mouth shut. It would have been far wiser if I had never made it . . . Should have known better than to put myself forward that way . . . Should have known they would choose me to go to England and plead our cause before the king. (*Dourly*) " 'Twould only be for a short time," they said. "Just a matter of a few months," they assured me. A few months! Eleven years! Eleven years I remained in England—except for one short visit home. First it was the Penn case. (*Plaintively*) Then, one thing after another . . . one thing after another. (*Pauses, with great seriousness*) And then . . . a greater issue . . . (PEOPLE *are heard offstage and coming closer.*) A far greater issue came up.

PEOPLE (*offstage, increasing in volume, as if approaching*): No taxation without representation! . . . No taxation without representation. (*Repeat, as if passing by and going off into the distance.*)

BEN (*softly*): No taxation without representation . . . I was in England then, but I could hear those voices across the sea; the voices of an aroused people demanding the rights of Englishmen.

MIRROR: And it was indeed something to make those haughty English lords pick up their ears, aye, Ben?

(*The lights, stage left go up.*)

BEN: I appeared before Parliament . . . tried to explain the feelings of my countrymen.

SCENE 7

FRANKLIN *is winding up a speech. He appears to be address-ing the members of the House of Commons, who are offstage and remain unseen. Seated behind him on a platform, slightly up front, is the* SPEAKER *of the House and the* SCRIBE, *who is taking notes of the proceedings.*

FRANKLIN: And so, members of the House of Commons, as a representative of His Majesty's colonies in America, I appeal to your good judgment, and beg you to repeal the Stamp Act!

(*There is an angry mutter among the members.*)

SPEAKER: Mr. Franklin, would you care to sumbit to an examination on this question?

FRANKLIN: It would afford me great pleasure, sir.

FIRST MEMBER (*offstage*): Question, Mr. Speaker! Question!

SPEAKER: Mr. Townley of Coventry.

FIRST MEMBER: Mr. Franklin, are not the colonies, from their circumstances, well able to pay the stamp duty?

FRANKLIN: In gold, as required? (*Shakes his head*) No, sir! In my opinion, sir, there is not gold enough in the colonies to pay the stamp duty for one year.

SECOND MEMBER (*offstage*): Question, Mr. Speaker!

SPEAKER: Mr. Snigby of Cornwall.

SECOND MEMBER: Mr. Franklin, do you deem it right that America should be protected by this country and pay no part of the expenses?

FRANKLIN: That is not the case, sir. The colonies raised, clothed and paid, during the last war against the French and Indians, near 25,000 men, and spent many millions of pounds.

THIRD MEMBER: Question, Mr. Speaker!

SPEAKER: Mr. Trevelyan of Manchester.

THIRD MEMBER: Mr. Franklin, do you think the people of America will submit to the Stamp Act?

FRANKLIN: No, never! (*An angry rumble rises in the House.*) Unless compelled to do so by force of arms!

FOURTH MEMBER: Then it *shall* be by force of arms! But submit they must!

(*The* SPEAKER *raps his gavel sharply as a commotion starts in the House.*)

SPEAKER (*sharply*): Mr. Trelawney . . . if you please, sir! (*Gavel*) Gentlemen! Gentlemen! (*The House subsides with an angry mutter in background.*)

FRANKLIN (*with quiet warning*). If those are your sentiments, sir, then let me warn you, gentlemen: America will meet force with force.

MEMBERS: Sedition! Sedition! That is naught but sedition! Treasonable words, Mr. Franklin!

(*The* SPEAKER *raps his gavel to restore order, then turns to* FRANKLIN *with incredulity in his tone.*)

SPEAKER: What mean you by those words, Mr. Franklin? Is it truly your belief that the colonies will revolt against the Crown?

FRANKLIN: Under circumstances of the most grievous tyranny and oppression, Mr. Speaker, that is possible. Aye, highly possible. (*Speaking over the loud rumble in the House*) Aye, mark me, gentlemen! The waves do not rise but when the wind blows! Your Stamp Act has caused a storm to rage over America! I urge you . . . I implore you . . . repeal the Stamp Act before that storm grows to a tempest!

(*With loud cries of "sedition" and "treason," and the rapping of the gravel over the* SPEAKER's *demand for order, scene fades to black, stage left.*)

BEN (*with grim satisfaction*): And they repealed it . . . indeed they did. (*Regretfully*) Ah, but there was no end to the provocations that the mother country heaped upon the colonies.

MIRROR: Which kept you in England, Ben.

BEN (*nods*): Doing the best I could to find a peaceful solution to the bad feeling between the colonies and England. (Sighs) But, I had to admit failure. And I knew, then, it had to be settled in the agony of blood and fire. (Broodingly) I returned home . . . heavy of heart . . . my mission a failure.

SCENE 8

DURING above, the light, stage left, goes up, and FRANKLIN, considerably aged, enters his workshop, followed closely by his daughter SALLY. FRANKLIN stands looking at his gadgets for a moment. His shoulders are slumped, his head bowed sadly as he longingly fingers his gadgets.

BEN: And Debby . . . my dear Debby . . . was dead . . . The old house seemed empty . . . cold . . . so cold without her. FRANKLIN runs his fingers over the surface of his workbench. He looks at his fingers, smiles sadly at the dust on his finger-tips.) Dust . . . dust . . . Dust over everything . . . even my poor Debby. (FRANKLIN turns his head to look lovingly at SALLY.) Thank heavens my daughter Sally was there to greet me upon my return home, after eleven years of absence.

SALLY (from stage left): Everything is just as you left it when you went away, father. Mother would not allow us to even dust in here. (FRANKLIN nods with a tender smile of appreciation and love.) You look so tired, father . . . you must rest now.

FRANKLIN (shaking his head sadly): Rest? Ah, dear child, there is no time for me to rest. For me or any of us here in America. (Longingly) And yet—how I long for it—how I long for it . . . to rest. To retire to my books, my garden . . . (Looks at workbench) and my experiments. (Turns away from the bench; speaks stronger, with determination and some bitterness) Nay, there shall be no rest, for there shall be no peace for sometime to come.

(SALLY pushes a chair forward for him and seats herself close to it.)

SALLY (trying to lighten his mood by speaking with anima-

tion): Come you now, sit down here, and tell me all about Europe (FRANKLIN *sits down.*) They say you were honored and acclaimed everywhere!

FRANKLIN (*smiling*): Yes, yes . . . I was presented at every court in Europe . . . dined with royalty . . . was elected to every scientific society on the continent. (*It all means just nothing to him now.*) Is that what you mean, dear?

SALLY: Oh, I'm so proud of you, father!

FRANKLIN (*smiling fondly*): Are you, dear? I am so glad.

SALLY: Is it true that the great William Pitt came to call upon you in London?

FRANKLIN: Quite so, he did call on me, several times. (*Amused*) You know, I greatly suspect that I remained a deep puzzle to that worthy gentleman for some time.

SALLY: Puzzle? How so?

FRANKLIN: Before I came to England the people there had the strangest misconceptions about us Colonials. They most probably expected me to appear before them in buckskin garb, with dozens of scalps dangling from my belt.

SALLY (*laughing gaily*): Not really!

FRANKLIN: But in time . . . in time they learned to respect me, and through me, developed a greater respect for all our countrymen. Yes, I have many friends in Europe, friends that will stand us in good stead when the proper time comes. And we will need friends. (*Wearily lifting himself from the chair*) And now, my dear, fetch me my cloak, I must be off.

SALLY (*protests*): Off? But . . . but you just arrived home! Where are you going?

FRANKLIN: My old friend, Colonel George Washington, has sent me a message, a message of great import. I have been chosen as delegate from Pennsylvania to the Continental Congress.

SALLY: But you are so worn from your journey. You must rest a day or so before—

FRANKLIN: No, Sally. Our country, I fear me, is preparing for war against England. Under those circumstances, can I refuse my services? (*As they walk off*) Aye, an old man I

may be, but they are welcome to what is left of me.
(*They exit, as stage left goes black. On stage right,* BEN, *with the help of his stick, rises painfully to his feet. He shuffles over to the bookcase and begins to peer at the books over the tops of his spectacles.*)

MIRROR: What are you looking for, Ben?

BEN: A book. (*Turns his head towards* MIRROR) Now, just don't go away. I'll be back. (*Turns back to books, pulls one out*) Ah, here it is . . . here it is. (*He shuffles back to chair, remains standing, and, leaning down to the light of the candle, begins turning the pages.*)

MIRROR: Is that a history book, Ben?

BEN: It is.

MIRROR: Could it be, perchance, something that Tom Jefferson wrote that you seek? Something he read to the delegates at the Continental Congress, here in Philadelphia?

BEN: (*peering at* MIRROR, *a bit crossly*): How did you know?

MIRROR: Oh, I don't find it very difficult to read your mind, you know. (BEN *is leafing through the book.*) You were there, Ben.

BEN: Yes, I was there. (*Finds the place*) Ah, here it is. (*His eyes on the page, murmurs*) This is the moment . . . the one moment in my life, I would fain relive . . .

MIRROR: But need you strain your poor old eyes, Ben? (*Whispers*) Listen, Ben . . . listen . . .

SCENE 9

During the above, an amber spot reveals THOMAS JEFFERSON *standing, stage left, holding a document in his hand.* BEN *stands and listens, stage right, as* JEFFERSON *reads from the Declaration of Independence. Occasionally* BEN *nods his head, a rapt expression on his face.*

JEFFERSON (*reads*): When in the course of human events, it becomes necessary for one people to dissolve the political bonds which have connected them with another, and to assume among the powers of the earth, the separate and equal station to which the Laws of Nature and of Nature's God entitle them, a decent respect to the opinions of mankind requires that they should declare the causes which impel them to the separation. (*Pauses.*)

BEN (*low, reverently*): Beautiful, Tom . . . beautiful . . .

JEFFERSON (*continues*): We hold these truths to be self-evident, that all men are created equal, that they are endowed by their Creator with certain unalienable Rights, that among these are Life, Liberty and the pursuit of Happiness. (*As* JEFFERSON *continues reading, the amber spot, stage left, dims down slowly and goes to black.* JEFFERSON's *voice gets lower as spot dims.*) That to secure these rights, Governments are instituted among Men, deriving their just powers from the consent of the governed. . . .

> (*As the scene stage left closes, and* JEFFERSON's *voice is not heard,* BEN, *stage right, is still lost in that great moment.*)

BEN (*his eyes cast down, slowly, with great solemnity*): And so . . . we mutually pledged to each other our lives, our fortunes . . . and our sacred honor. And it was so we declared our independence from England. (*He straightens up slowly, turns and walks back to the bookcase, replaces the book, his hand lingering lovingly on the binding. He walks back to his chair, remains standing.*) But these truths . . . these rights . . . had to be bought and paid for with blood. (*As the light, stage left, starts going up*) Two harrowing years . . . two harrowing years went by. We lacked supplies. We lacked money. It was truly a time to try men's souls.

SCENE 10

On stage left, a group of five PATRIOTS is huddled around a fire in the open. They are tattered and cold, with blankets and old greatcoats draped over their shoulders. Three of them have their feet bound in old sackings. Their muskets are stacked close by. TOM PAINE is seated slightly in front of the

group, one leg drawn up under him, writing on a paper
which rests upon a drum-head. PAINE appears to have finished
writing. He places his quill down, picks up the paper. He
reads the opening lines to himself, low, but audibly. One of
the PATRIOTS turns his head to listen.)

PAINE: These are the times that try men's souls . . . The
summer soldier and the sunshine patriot . . . (He stops to
pick up his quill, makes a correction.)

FIRST PATRIOT: What be you writing there, Mr. Paine?

PAINE (smiles): Oh, just a bit of common sense, I trust . . .
which I hope to see printed.

SECOND PATRIOT: Common sense? Was that not the title of
a pamphlet you writ, sir . . . in '76, or thereabouts?

PAINE: It was, soldier.

SECOND PATRIOT: I recall it well, sir . . . 'deed I do! Some do
say, it was a right powerful influence in bringing about
Independence in '76.

PAINE: It may have helped at that. (Sighs) I can only hope
that this message of mine will strengthen the hearts of
our people with courage to carry on in these trying times.

THIRD PATRIOT (morosely): Meaning no offense, Mr. Paine,
but if ye were to ask the likes of me, we could do more
with a bit of food in our bellies, so's we can carry on.

PAINE (good-humoredly): Now, friend, you wouldn't want
to sell your birthright . . . your birthright of freedom for
a mess of pottage, would you?

THIRD PATRIOT: Hah! If ye would have me take my choice
twixt a mess of pottage . . . (Points to paper) or a pot of
message . . . then, sir—(PAINE laughs at his quip.)

FOURTH PATRIOT (sharply): Silas Hubbs, if you'd jest shut
that big clabbermouth of yours for a spell, mebbe Mr.
Paine would favor us with a readin' of his message.

THIRD PATRIOT (grumbles): Meant no offense. Just plumb
gut-shrunk, is all.

FOURTH PATRIOT: Will you read it us, Mr. Paine?

PAINE: Be pleased to, my friend.

(He leans closer to the firelight to read. In the midst of

his reading, GENERAL GEORGE WASHINGTON appears. He stands at a distance from the group, listening to PAINE intently. The PATRIOTS are so absorbed in the message, they are entirely unaware of his presence.)

PAINE: These are the times that try men's souls. The summer soldier and the sunshine patriot will, in this crisis, shrink from the service of their country; but he that stands it now deserves the love and thanks of man and woman. (WASHINGTON enters.) Tyranny, like hell, is not easily conquered; yet we have this consolation with us, that the harder the conflict, the more glorious the triumph. What we obtain too cheap, we esteem too lightly: it is—
(The THIRD PATRIOT sees WASHINGTON. He nudges FOURTH PATRIOT and quickly scrambles to his feet. WASHINGTON with a motion of his hand urges them to sit down, but it is too late. PAINE stops reading and rises. WASHINGTON, with a regretful expression walks closer to the fire.)

WASHINGTON (with humbleness and sincere regret): I'm terribly sorry, Tom. Please forgive me for interrupting. It would have pleased me to hear it through.
(PAINE rolls up the document and extends it to WASHINGTON with a respectful bow.)

PAINE: May I offer you it to read at your leisure, General Washington? And if you, perchance, deem it worthy for publication . . .

WASHINGTON (taking the paper): Thank you, Tom. From the little I heard, it may be just what is needed in these— as you so well have penned— ". . . times that try men's souls."
(Drums roll offstage sounding the muster call. The PATRIOTS move quickly to their stacked muskets. PAINE starts to move for his musket, stops, looks toward WASHINGTON for permission. As the PATRIOTS rush off on the double, WASHINGTON motions PAINE to stay.)

WASHINGTON: Just a muster call to receive an issue of ammunition that has but arrived—finally, thank the Lord— and Mr. Franklin.

(BEN, *on stage right, cocks an eyebrow with a "Well, what-do-you-know" expression directed at the* MIRROR.)

PAINE: Mr. Franklin, sir?

WASHINGTON (nods): Aye, Mr. Franklin. As you may know, he has been stationed in France for some time now, pleading our cause. And that, most eloquently, judging by the shipment of arms and money we are beginning to receive from France.

PAINE: I, *personally*, have much to thank Mr. Franklin for, General Washington.

WASHINGTON: Oh, have you?

PAINE: It was he who found me poor and destitute in London in the year '74, and gave me letters of introduction to many of his friends, who kindly helped me get established in Philadelphia. So, General, if I have been of any help in furthering our cause, we can thank the good Mr. Franklin for that too.

WASHINGTON: Indeed we must. For, in my mind, you have been worth as much as a regiment of Continentals, Tom.

PAINE: You honor me much too much, General Washington.

WASHINGTON: By no means. (*Smiles as he looks off right*) Your pen may be mightier than the sword, Tom Paine, but I can't say 'twould do the cause any harm if you filled your powder horn and shot bag with ammunition, before it is all gone.

PAINE (*bows*): By your leave, General Washington.

(*After* PAINE *has gone,* WASHINGTON *unrolls the manuscript, leans closer to the firelight and begins reading it to himself. Occasionally he nods with approval. He begins to roll up the manuscript.*)

WASHINGTON (*low*): A good lad . . . a good lad, that Thomas Paine . . .

(*He turns and begins to walk off, as stage left dims and goes to black.*)

BEN (*firmly*): A good lad *indeed*, that Thomas Paine. I made no mistake about him, when I saw him in London. There was genius in his eyes, that's why I packed him off to America.

MIRROR: And when the struggle was over, Ben . . . ?

BEN: And we were a free and independent nation . . . (*Deeply aggrieved*) You would think then, wouldn't you, that they would allow me to come home? But no! They kept me in France as America's first Ambassador abroad. And there I remained for nine years more. Nine long years!

MIRROR: But the nation needed you there, Ben.

BEN: And when I finally did come home . . .

MIRROR (*chuckles*): They elected you President of the State of Pennsylvania.

BEN: Not once, but thrice—thrice, mind you! Aye, they ate my flesh, then they picked my old bones. (*Plaintively*) And all I wished to do was get to my books . . . my garden . . . my experiments . . . (*Determined, demands*) What day is this?

MIRROR (*thinking*): Mmm . . . April the 17, 1790, Ben.

(BEN *taps the floor with his stick, expressing absolute determination.*)

BEN: Now, you mark me! This day . . . this very day, I mean to retire! And no one—no one on God's earth will make me change my mind!

(*He settles himself painfully in his chair, leans back with a tired sigh.*)

MIRROR (*tenderly*): Aye, Ben . . . today you will retire . . . retire to a well deserved rest.

(BEN's *eyes close. The hand that holds the stick dangles over the side of the chair.*)

MIRROR: Aye, close your eyes, Ben . . . Close your eyes and rest . . . rest . . .

(*As the curtain begins to descend, we see* BEN's *hand release the stick, which quietly falls to the floor.*)

CURTAIN

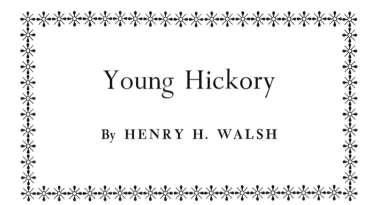

Young Hickory

By HENRY H. WALSH

YOUNG HICKORY

CHARACTERS: 9 males; 1 female;
as many extras as desired in Scene 3

PLAYING TIME: 45 minutes

SETS: Five

✍ Historical Notes

IN CREATING the character of Andrew Jackson as a boy, I drew upon several incidents in the turbulent and colorful career of "Old Hickory"—the man, the soldier, and the President. As a man he hated orders and those who ordered; he was fretful under discipline, hasty of temper, quick to take offense, violent in behavior, and implacable in his hatreds.

Judging the man, we wonder if it would have made any difference to him if he *had* known that peace with Britain had been signed, and the War of 1812 ended, when he attacked the British army in New Orleans on January 8, 1815, handing them a decisive defeat. Be this as it may, his act made the fiery, imperious Jackson a tremendous hero and set him on the road to the White House.

As Major General Jackson, in 1817 he disobeyed the orders of his superiors by refusing to disband his troops, and instead attacked the Spanish in Florida (with whom the United States was not at war). While about it, he executed two British subjects in Pensacola who, he claimed, were stirring up the Indians. This last may have delighted him no end, but could have gotten this country into another war with Great Britain. He was involved in several bloody duels, and expressed deep regret toward the end of his Presidency that "he had never had an opportunity to shoot Clay or hang Calhoun." And yet he was capable of a passionate, deep, and abiding love for a woman—Rachel, his wife.

Andrew Jackson was born March 15, 1767, near Waxhaw Creek in what is now Lancaster County, South Carolina, on the border of North Carolina. His father, Andrew Jackson, was a poor farmer of Scots-Irish descent who had emigrated from Ireland, bringing with him his wife, Elizabeth Hutchinson Jackson, a woman of courage and strong character. They had three sons—Hugh, Robert, and Andrew who was born a few days after his father died. The Widow Jackson carried on, coping with all the hardships of a frontier life.

During the Revolutionary War, all three of Elizabeth's sons saw active fighting. Hugh, the oldest, died in the battle at Hanging Rock. Robert was captured and died on the journey home after being released, through Elizabeth's intercession, from a British war prison where he had contracted smallpox. Andrew was taken by the British and suffered a severe saber wound when he refused to black an officer's boots. Elizabeth returned to the British prison camp to nurse the American prisoners of war, where she died of smallpox. It is not hard to understand why Andrew Jackson maintained a lasting hatred for the British. These early experiences determined his conduct and character, creating a strong sense of individuality and a personality that makes the name of "Old Hickory" stand out in bold type in the story of America.

⋪ Production Notes

⟨ Characters

ELIZABETH JACKSON, *mother of Andrew and Robert Jackson*
ANDREW JACKSON, *Elizabeth's youngest son*
ROBERT JACKSON, *Elizabeth's second son*
ANGUS MACPHERSON, *a backwoods peddler*
BUSHWHACKER, *a Tory marauder, an offstage voice*
DOCTOR COLDEN, *an American army surgeon*
FIRST PATRIOT
JEB CRAWFORD, *Elizabeth's nephew*
SECOND PATRIOT
LORD RAWDEN, *a British general*
CAPTAIN FURNESS, *aide-de-camp to Lord Rawden*

⟨ Scenes

SCENE 1: The Jackson cabin in the backwoods of South Carolina in the spring of 1779.

SCENE 2: A stone wall bordering an open field. Time about ten days later.

SCENE 3: Interior of a barn being used as a field hospital, the same time as SCENE 2.

SCENE 4: The headquarters of Lord Rawden in Camden, South Carolina, several days later.

SCENE 5: A section of the British prison camp in Camden, South Carolina, fifteen minutes later.

⟨ Settings

SCENE 1: The interior of a backwoods log cabin. A fieldstone fireplace, centered on the left wall. Exit to another room, left back. A heavily barred door, right. Two small windows

93

in the back wall. Table and benches, center stage. Cupboard, left back. 2 wooden chairs. SCENE 2: Pasture wall in an open field. SCENE 3: Interior of a barn. Several straw pallets on the barn floor. SCENE 4: British command headquarters. Desk and chair, left center. Two other chairs are near the desk, and a British flag hangs on the wall behind it. Entrance, right. SCENE 5: Section of British war prison interior. Two straw pallets, left center.

❨ Costumes

SCENE 1: Andy and Robbie Jackson wear deerskin breeches, fustian shirts, buckskin jerkins, and moccasins. Elizabeth is dressed in a simple Colonial gown, long-skirted and tight-bodiced, with a long apron covering her dress. Angus wears a deerskin jacket and heavy homespuns. His breeches are tucked into high-laced moccasins. On his head he wears a woolen cap. SCENE 2: Andy and Robbie wear deerskin jackets and the previous dress. Fur hats or woolen stocking hats on their heads. SCENE 3: Elizabeth wears the same clothing as before, plus a heavy cape. Dr. Colden is in his shirtsleeves. His sleeves are rolled up and he wears a waistcoat. The patriots are dressed like the Jackson boys. SCENE 4: Lord Rawden and Captain Furness are in British regimentals: red coats, light breeches, high boots, etc. SCENE 5: Elizabeth, Andy and Robbie are dressed as before.

❨ Properties

SCENE 1: Table, benches, chairs, cupboard, dishes and iron pot, spoons, etc., bowls, ladle, 4 rifles, powderhorns and shot pouches, ramrods, female garments, chest, shears, saddlebags. SCENE 2: No additional properties. SCENE 3: Piles of hay as beds, several blankets, strips of cloth for bandages. SCENE 4: Desk, 3 chairs, two swords, British flag, papers, inkhorn and quill. SCENE 5: 2 straw pallets, 2 blankets, water pail and dipper.

◖ Lighting

Scene 1: daylight. Scene 2: daylight in an open field. Scene 3: daylight, but quite dim, entering from right entrance unseen. Scene 4: bright daylight. Scene 5: murky interior daylight.

(Note: The musket shots, in Scene 1, can be handled off-stage with blank cartridges, synchronized with the action on stage. The rattle of musketry, in Scene 2, can be simulated off-stage with drumsticks on the side of a drum.)

Scene II - "Young Hickory"

Young Hickory

SCENE 1

The interior of the Jackson cabin on a late afternoon in the year 1779. One room is visible, with an open doorway, left back, leading to another room. To the left of this doorway, facing front, is a dish closet. A broad fieldstone fireplace is centered in the left wall. A black iron cooking pot hangs in the fireplace. On the hearth: irons, bellows, cooking utensils, etc. A hand-hewn trestle table and two backless benches are center stage. Flat-backed wooden chairs on either side of the fireplace. A heavily-barred door right center leads to the outside. Daylight enters through two highly placed windows in the back wall.

At curtain rise, ANDY, aged 12, and ROBBIE, aged 14, pause in the midst of a military drill to engage in an argument. They stand face to face, holding muskets butt down on the floor. They wear powderhorns and shot-pouches dangling from broad belts. ANDY, his head thrust forward belligerently is scowling at ROBBIE.

ANDY: Poppycock! I say all this drilling is just a mess of gol-darned poppycock!
ROBBIE (sternly): Poppycock . . . sir!
ANDY (puzzled): Huh?
ROBBIE: When you address your superior officer, say "sir"!
(ELIZABETH enters from the other room during the above, carrying three pewter plates and spoons. She starts setting the table for supper. She casts an affectionate, amused smile on her two boys, then turns and exits left.)
ANDY (through clenched teeth): I still think this drilling is just gol-darned poppycock . . . captain, sir, sir, SIR!

97

ROBBIE (*scathingly*): I reckon you think you know more about warring than Brother Hugh or Colonel Davie, huh?

ANDY: I can place a ball through the eye of a squirrel at two hundred paces, can't I . . . can't I, now?

ROBBIE: That has nothing to do with it! If we're going to join up with Colonel Davie's fighters, you got to learn soldiering . . . and there's more to soldiering than just shooting straight.

(ELIZABETH *enters again carrying three bowls in her hand. She sets them down on the hearth and starts ladling food into the bowls from the fireplace pot.*)

ANDY (*wearily*): Like as what? Like as this mess—

ROBBIE (*interrupting firmly*): Discipline! That's what a soldier has to learn . . . discipline!

ANDY (*his jaw thrust forward*): Ain't no one going to make me—

ROBBIE (*sharply*): Silence in the ranks! (ANDY *glares at him, holds his tongue with difficulty.* ROBBIE *snaps an order.*) Present . . . arms! (ROBBIE *presents arms.* ANDY, *with a scowl, follows suit.*) Shoulder . . . arms! (*Both shoulder arms,* ROBBIE *wheels around smartly on his heel, his back to* ANDY.) For-rrerd march! (ANDY *steps forward with the wrong foot, tramples on* ROBBIE's *heel, almost trips him.*) You puddin'-headed oaf! If you ain't the clumsiest . . .

ANDY (*belligerently*): Don't you go calling me a . . . a puddin'-head, Robert Jackson!

(ELIZABETH *is at the table now, arranging the settings. She looks up.*)

ELIZABETH: Now, now, Andy, control that temper of yours. Anyway, it's time to stop playing and set for supper.

(ANDY *and* ROBBIE *forget their difference and unite against the felt slight to their manhood.*)

ANDY and ROBBIE (*together indignantly*): Playing?

ROBBIE: We're not playing, ma. Any day now we'll be off to join up with Brother Hugh and Colonel Davie to fight the Redcoats . . . and Andy here has got to learn some soldiering.

ELIZABETH (*hiding a smile*): Well now, can't do any fighting on an empty stomach . . . so set.

(*They walk up to the table glumly.*)

ANDY: You wouldn't want us Jacksons to stay home while there's a war going on, would you now? Got to uphold the honor of the Jacksons, don't we?

ELIZABETH (*sadly amused*): Suppose you let Brother Hugh uphold the honor of the family for the time being, Andy lad. Time enough for you both to do a mite of growing up before you go off to war.

ROBBIE: Aw, ma . . .

ELIZABETH (*firmly but kindly*): Now put by your muskets and set. (*The boys rest their muskets against the wall and sit down, as* ELIZABETH *smiles at them.*) Anyway, you wouldn't want to leave your poor ma all alone in the wilderness without a man to protect her, would you? (*Seriously*) What with all those bands of Tories roaming the Waxhaw countryside . . .

ROBBIE: Tories? They be nothing but a band of thieving, murdering bushwhackers, that's all they are. Aye, pretending to be Loyalists, so they can steal and pillage the settlers while the menfolk are away to the war.

ELIZABETH: I guess you're right, Robbie lad, that's all they are indeed. (*Sadly*) They ran off the Stockwell's horses yestereve, and burned . . . (*She stops, looks down at her plate, then looks up at* ROBBIE *promptingly.*) Robbie?

(*They bow their heads for grace.*)

ROBBIE: Bless, O Father, Thy gifts to our use and us to Thy service; for Thy sake, Amen. (*They lift their heads and start to eat.* ROBBIE *chuckles.*)

ANDY (*still grumpy*): What you chuckling at, Robbie Jackson?

ROBBIE: I just minded something Nulachucky Jack said when he came by a fortnight ago. I asked him did he say grace, seeing as how he's married to a Cherokee squaw, and living most time with the Indians, 'way he does. (*Imitates Jack*) "Lad," he says, "Pray? Ah sure does . . . and prays hard! Not to thank the Lord, mind ye . . . but to ask Him to give me the strength to survive them vittles that squaw woman of mine sets before me!" (*Their laughter is suddenly interrupted when* ROBBIE, *with a tense look on his face, lifts his palm.*) Hush!

ANDY: What for you say hush . . . ?

ROBBIE (*low*): Hush, I say! I think I hear something stirring outside the door! (*They wait in tense silence, their eyes fastened on the door.*)

ANDY: I don't hear—

    (*There is a loud thumping on the door. The three spring to their feet and rush for their muskets.* ELIZABETH *grabs hers from the wall.*)

BUSHWHACKER (*voice outside*): Open up, you rebels!

ROBBIE: Bushwhackers!

ELIZABETH (*lifting her musket*): Be off, ye murdering monsters!

BUSHWHACKER: Hand me that ax, Proudy!

ANDY: Ma . . . it . . . it's a whole band of bushwhackers, ma!

ELIZABETH (*leveling her musket at the door*): Andy, open the door . . . AND STAND *CLEAR!*

ANDY (*astonished, frightened*): But . . . but, ma!

ELIZABETH: Do like I say, son! (*As* ANDY *moves to obey.*) Robbie, you hold your fire 'till I tell you to shoot!

    (ELIZABETH *and* ROBBIE *stand with their muskets leveled at the door as* ANDY *slips the bolt, flings the door open, jumping behind it as he does so.* ELIZABETH *shoots.*)

ELIZABETH: Fire, Robbie! (ROBBIE *shoots.*)

BUSHWHACKER: Run for it, men! Run for the horses! There's a nest of rebels in there!

ELIZABETH: Shut the door, Andy! (ANDY *doesn't obey her command. He rushes to the open door and brings his musket up to shoot.* ELIZABETH *yells at him.*) Andy, no! Stand clear, I say! (ANDY *shoots, then quickly slams the door and bolts it.*)

ROBBIE: You . . . you get one, Andy?

ANDY (*greatly vexed*): Pshaw, no! I woulda though, if ma hadn't yelled at me then!

ROBBIE (*disappointed*): Guess we didn't get a-one of them then.

ELIZABETH: They were crouching beside the door when we fired, Robbie. (*Sternly*) And now . . . as for you, Andy! Didn't you hear me tell you—

ANDY (*suddenly alarmed*): Ma! Do you reckon they'll run off with our horses?

ELIZABETH (*with sad resignation*): They may just do that, son. But there's nothing we can do—(*Stops as* ANDY *runs to the door to open it.*) No, Andy! No! (*She rushes after him to grab his arm.*)

ANDY: No thieving, stinking polecat is going to . . . Ma, please let me—

ELIZABETH: Let them take the horses, lad.

ANDY: But, ma . . . !

ELIZABETH: No, Andy, I won't have you sacrificing your life for them. We'll get by—

(*They hear a musket shot off, freeze for a moment.*)

ROBBIE: What was that shot, ma?

ELIZABETH: It was a shot, wasn't it?

ROBBIE: You—you think maybe they be coming back?

ELIZABETH (*grimly*): No, but if they do, we'd better be ready for them. Reload your muskets, lads. (*She takes down her powderhorn and shot-bag from the peg and starts to reload. Her boys follow suit.*)

ANDY: Let them just try! We'll learn them . . . and learn them good, won't we Robbie?

(*They start at a loud knock on the door.*)

ANGUS (*outside*): Mrs. Jackson! It's me, Angus MacPherson!

ALL THREE: Angus! . . . Angus MacPherson! . . . It's Angus! (ELIZABETH *walks to the door and opens it.* ANGUS *comes sidling in, his musket on the ready, looking outdoors.* ELIZABETH *quickly closes the door and bolts it.*)

ELIZABETH: God's mercy, Mr. MacPherson, Providence must have directed your steps to our door!

ANDY and ROBBIE (*with a gush of words*): The bushwackers came down on us! . . . They were going to chop down the door! . . . We gave it to them good, we did! . . . You should have seen them run! And, ma—

ELIZABETH (*with a laugh*): Hold your clack, lads! La, what

101

an unholy clatter, and Mr. MacPherson barely a foot through the door.

ANDY: Our horses! They must have—

ANGUS: Ha' na fear, lad. They dinna take your horses. They were aboot to, but . . . (*He holds up his musket.*)

ROBBIE: That was you that shot then? (ANGUS *nods with a broad grin.*)

ROBBIE: Lawdy, 'tis good you happened along just then!

ANGUS: Weell now . . . I just dinna hoppen along, Robbie. Been trailing that band of cutthroats good part of the afternoon. When I saw them headed for your clearing, I cut through the woods and circled around to get here before they did, to warn ye. (*With a smile at the boys.*) Now if I had kenned that ye had two bra' men to home, Mrs. Jackson, I would na ha' worrit a-tall.

> (ANDY *throws his shoulders back proudly.* ROBBIE, *embarrassed, shuffles his feet; but he wears a pleased grin.* ELIZABETH *looks at them proudly.*)

ELIZABETH: Fetch another bowl, Robbie. Come set and sup with us, Mr. MacPherson.

ANGUS: Thankee, Mrs. Jackson.

> (ANGUS *sets his musket down against the wall, as* ROBBIE *goes into the other room to get a bowl and spoon.* ANDY *fetches a chair and places it at one end of the table.* ELIZABETH *is stirring the pot in the fireplace as the talk goes on.*)

ANDY: We never expected to see you in these parts Mr. MacPherson.

> (ROBBIE *appears with the bowl; he hands it to his mother; she begins to ladle some food into it.*)

ANGUS: And why not, lad? It's my worrk, isn't it . . . bringing folks in the backwoods the things they need?

ANDY (*bluntly*): But with a war going on, I would think you'd be shouldering a musket . . . 'stead of a peddler's pack.

ELIZABETH (*sharply*): Andy!

ANGUS (*smiling*): Ach, Mrs. Jackson, dinna scold the lad. I'm no offended. Couldna expect him to know.

ELIZABETH (*sternly to* ANDY): Angus is doing more for the American cause than any ten—

ANGUS (*cautions*): Hush, good woman.

ROBBIE: Oho! You old swamp fox! I'll wager you carry more in your head than you do in your peddler's pack, aye?

ANGUS (*sternly*): Perhaps. But, one thing I do na carry in my head, lad, is a loose tongue.

ELIZABETH: And let that be a caution to you, you clatterbox.

ROBBIE (*very contrite*): Sorry, Mr. MacPherson.

ANGUS: Na, na, lad . . . no harm done.

(*They sit down to the table and begin to eat.*)

ELIZABETH: What news of the war, Mr. MacPherson?

ANGUS (*gravely*): The war has come to the Waxhaw, Mrs. Jackson. Aye, 'tis more than cowardly bushwhackers ye have to fear now. (*As they look up at him inquiringly*) The British have landed in Charlestown—

ELIZABETH (*disturbed*): They have?

ANGUS: Aye, and they'll soon be down upon the Waxhaw.

ANDY (*cocksure*): Ho, not if Colonel Davie and his Carolina men have anything to say about it! Aye, Davie will drive every last one of those blasted Lobsterbacks into the sea! (*Proudly*) Perhaps you forget that Brother Hugh is with Davie! Why, if they as much as dare come this way, Brother Hugh will—

ANGUS (*with firmness, but kindly*): Hush, lad, and listen to old Angus MacPherson for a wee bit. (*Pauses*) I come from Davie's camp with news that will not gladden your hearts, but 'tis best ye know . . . (*He pauses.*)

ELIZABETH: What is it, good man?

ANGUS (*finding it hard*): Colonel Davie . . . has been routed by the British. (*There's a long, shocked pause.*)

ANDY: Nay, that could not be!

ANGUS: We were outnumbered, five to one. Davie's forces are, at this moment, in full retreat, and many a brave lad has fallen.

ELIZABETH (*anxiously*): Have you . . . have you heard of my son Hugh? Was he with . . . ?

ANGUS: I had no time to tarry or inquire after those I ken,

Mrs. Jackson. Colonel Davie dispatched me with a message to you people of the Waxhaw.

ELIZABETH: Aye?

ANGUS: In short, that he canna possibly hope to reorganize his forces this side of Hanging Rock—and Davie wants every male who can carry a gun to join him there. For there he means to make a stand. Aye, the outcome of that battle will settle the fate of the Waxhaw, for it will be them—or us.

ANDY (*looking at* ROBBIE): Every male who can carry a gun. Why, that means me—me and Robbie. Aye, Robbie? (ROBBIE *nods.*) Mr. MacPherson, where—?

ELIZABETH (*harshly*): Hush, Andrew!

ANDY (*protesting*): I can handle a musket good as any. I can place a ball—

ELIZABETH: Hush, I say! You are only a child—barely thirteen!

ANDY: Maybe so, but I can shoot, ma, and that's all they are looking for!

(ANGUS *is looking at* ANDY *and* ROBBIE *speculatively.* ELIZABETH *catches his look with growing horror.*)

ELIZABETH: Why . . . why are you looking at my young ones like that, Mr. MacPherson?

ROBBIE (*eagerly*): Ma, you heard what he said. Colonel Davie—

ELIZABETH: Hold your tongue! (*As* ANDY *is about to speak.*) Both of you! (*She rises in agitation.*) For shame, Mr. MacPherson!

ANGUS (*dropping his eyes*): Ach, my dear woman—

ELIZABETH: Putting rash thoughts like that in the heads of mere children!

ANDY and ROBBIE (*indignantly*): Children?!

ELIZABETH: Hold your tongues, I say! (*Turning to* ANGUS, *her lips tight, her eyes narrowed*) And if that's what you came to my door for, Angus MacPherson . . .

ANGUS (*rather unconvincingly*): By the bones of me old mother who lies these many years 'neath the sod in Achna-cloich, I swear I had na such thoughts in me mind!

ELIZABETH (*looking at him doubtfully*): Hmmm . . . (*Sadly*) Nay, this wilderness took my dear husband. Aye, that was hard . . . hard. But these are blows . . . hardships that every mortal must bear. These and other hardships, that our children may have a fair chance in this new land, and not die before their time. And Hugh—my son Hugh— only the good Lord knows what fate he has suffered. For aught we know, he . . . he may be lying sore wounded . . . or cold in some bloody field . . .

ROBBIE (*deeply affected*): Oh, ma! Ma, don't . . . don't take on so.

ELIZABETH: If only I knew . . . if only . . . (*Stops*) Mr. MacPherson . . .

ANGUS: Aye?

ELIZABETH: Did you bring those scissors I bade you fetch when you came by this way?

    (ANGUS *rises, glad to change the subject.*)

ANGUS: Aye, that I did! And the finest pair of shears ever factored in Glasgow! (*Walks toward door*) They be in my pack outside.

    (*As her two sons look at her questioningly,* ANGUS *walks to the door, stops, walks back to pick up his musket, returns to the door, opens it and peers out cautiously before he exits.*)

ELIZABETH (*indicating the chest in the corner*): Robbie, fetch me my garments from the chest there.

ROBBIE: Your . . . your garments, ma?

ELIZABETH: Aye, all of them. I mean to cut them into bandages.

    (ANGUS *appears with the shears in his hand. He closes the door.* ROBBIE *is at the chest gathering up dresses in his arms.*)

ANGUS: Here be your shears, ma'm.

ELIZABETH (*with a motion toward the other room*): My saddlebags, Andy. I'm leaving for Hanging Rock, and that, immediately.

ANGUS (*shaking his head*): Ah, me. 'Tis indeed a dangerous and foolhardy venture, woman. The streams are that swollen with the spring floods, and the roads heavily patrolled by the British.

(ANDY *places her saddlebags on the table, as* ROBBIE *dumps her clothing down beside them.*)

ELIZABETH: I'll get through. I need to.

ANGUS (*sighs*): Then may the Lord keep you and bring you back safely. (ELIZABETH *notes* ANDY's *woeful expression.*)

ELIZABETH (*with a reassuring smile*): Now, now, Andy lad, don't look so concerned, I'll be quite safe.

ANDY: It ain't that, ma. It . . . it's just that I want to go too.

ELIZABETH: Now, Andy!

ANDY: Please, ma!

ELIZABETH: You're to stay at home—both of you! Robbie will look after you.

(*She places her shears in the saddlebags, ties the dresses into a bundle.*)

ANDY (*grumbling*): Don't need no looking after.

(*She gets her cloak and puts it on.*)

ANGUS: If you could wait until the morrow, Mrs. Jackson . . . (ELIZABETH *shakes her head firmly.*) I would ride with you to Hanging Rock.

ELIZABETH (*picking up the bundle*): You have your own mission to complete, and I have mine. Neither one can wait.

ANGUS (*relieving her of the bundle*): Ah, laddies, a braver heart never beat. (*She gathers up her musket and saddlebags.*) I'll ride with you to Ten Mile Creek and see you across the stream. (*She is about to protest.*) It won't take me out of my way, woman!

ELIZABETH (*turning to her sons*): Now, be good lads. (*Her sons look glumly at her.*) Oh, come now, kiss your ma goodby. (*They kiss her.*) And if by any chance I'm not back within a fortnight, make your way to Aunt Jane Crawford's plantation. (*Pointedly*) And I want you to remain there until I get back. Is that clear? (*Their nod is hardly perceptible, which causes her to look at them keenly. Then she turns and walks to the door.*)

ROBBIE: Take care, ma . . . and . . . and come back soon.

ELIZABETH: Don't you worry now. Your ma knows how to take care of herself.

ANDY: Goodbye, ma!

ELIZABETH (*as she exits followed by* ANGUS): Goodbye, lads!

ANGUS: God be with ye, laddies.

ANDY and ROBBIE: Goodbye, Mr. MacPherson.

(*When they have gone, the boys look at the door silently for a moment, then* ROBBIE *turns to* ANDY *with a determined thrust to his jaw.*)

ROBBIE: Fetch the lard can, Andy, and start cleaning the muskets.

ANDY (*wide-eyed*): Robbie . . . you mean . . . ?

ROBBIE: Aye, as soon as they get beyond the turn, we'll saddle up the ponies. We're heading for Davie's camp at Hanging Rock!

(ANDY *hastens toward the muskets.*)

SCENE 2

A pasture wall bordering an open field; ten days later. During curtain rise, shots sound in the far distance. Then ROBBIE *and* ANDY *come running in from the left, crouching low. They duck behind the wall, lying flat on their stomachs.*

ROBBIE (*with great satisfaction*): Those redcoats sure make prime targets, don't they, Andy?

ANDY: Did you do for that last one, Robbie . . . did you?

ROBBIE: No-o-o . . . not exactly.

ANDY (*incredulous*): You mean you missed?

ROBBIE (*indignantly*): Missed? Since when do us Jacksons miss what we're sighting at! I hit what was showing. Couldn't do more'n that, could I now?

ANDY: What were he a-showin', Robbie?

ROBBIE (*chuckles*): His coattails.

ANDY (*chuckles*): Guess that be one set of pants won't be setting down for a long, long time, aye, Robbie?

(ANDY *lifts his head above the wall, as* ROBBIE *is in the act of ramming a ball down the muzzle of his musket.*)

ROBBIE (*sharply*): Keep down, you dang fool! Want to get a ball through your head, do you?

ANDY (*grumbling*): I just wanted to see where that—

ROBBIE: You keep your head down like I tell you, or I'll larrup you with this ramrod, so help me, I will! . . . Hand me your powderhorn.

ANDY: Won't do you a mite of good.

ROBBIE (*shocked*): Empty?

ANDY: Not a grain. Just about to ask you to pass me your'n.

ROBBIE: Tarnation! No sense in our staying here then.

ANDY (*lifting his head*): Robbie, look yonder! (ROBBIE *smacks him with his ramrod.* ANDY *yelps.*) Owww . . .

ROBBIE: Didn't I tell you I'd larrup you?

ANDY: But . . . but there's a whole mess of Redcoats coming up!

(ROBBIE *lifts his head cautiously.*)

ROBBIE: I see them. Lor-a-me, lined up as if they were parading. If we only had some powder!

ANDY: Well, we haven't any, so we better git, and git fast!

ROBBIE: Run for the brush yonder, but keep your head down. (*Crouching low, they start to run. We hear a shot go off.* ANDY, *with a cry of pain, stumbles and remains on the ground clutching his leg.* ROBBIE *turns and runs back to him.*)

ANDY: My . . . my leg, Robbie . . .

ROBBIE: You . . . you get hit, Andy?

ANDY (*groans*): My leg.

ROBBIE: Lemme see . . .

ANDY: No, Robbie, run! Run for it or you'll be cotched by the Redcoats!

ROBBIE: No, Andy! Ma told me to mind you!

ANDY: No sense in your being took, Robbie!

ROBBIE: I'm not letting you out of my sight! (*Looks to the right behind him*) Too late, anyway. We'll never make the brush now. They're coming up behind us.

REDCOAT (*offstage*): Drop that musket, rebel! (*As* ROBBIE *hesitates*) Drop it, I say, or I'll fire!

ROBBIE (*dropping his musket*): All right, you bloody Lobsterbacks, come and take us!

SCENE 3

The same time as Scene 2. The interior of a barn not far
from the fighting front at Hanging Rock. The barn is being
used as an emergency field hospital for the wounded patriots.
Wounded soldiers, covered with blankets, are lying on beds
of hay. Front stage, ELIZABETH and DR. COLDEN attend a
wounded soldier who has just been brought in. COLDEN
is kneeling by his side as ELIZABETH stands by holding bandages and her shears in her hands.

FIRST PATRIOT (painfully): Consarn those blasted Regulars!
(With grudging admiration) They can handle their weap-
ons a sight better than we reckoned.

COLDEN: Lie still, man, while I get that ball out of your arm.
(To ELIZABETH) Cut away his breecher leg, ma'm, and
see to that wound.

(ELIZABETH kneels, is about to use her shears.)

FIRST PATRIOT (grins, despite his pain): You'll find buckskin
too tough for them shears, ma'm. (He draws his hunting
knife from the sheath strapped to his belt.) Here, use my
knife. (He restrains a groan as the doctor probes.) Mmm
—mm!

(ELIZABETH is working on his leg.)

COLDEN: There, that's out. Wash out the wound and bandage it up, Mrs. Jackson. Now let me look to his leg.

ELIZABETH: The ball went right through, Doctor Colden.

COLDEN: Good. Save him the pain of probing for it.

ELIZABETH: I'll finish up with this lad, Doctor Colden. (Motions toward the back) There's a lad there badly hit.

COLDEN (soberly): Aye, there's many of them badly hit.
(Amazed) Never saw the likes of it. Hardly a man here
with less than two wounds.

(ELIZABETH is bandaging the wounds.)

FIRST PATRIOT: We aimed to hold that crossing until help
came.

COLDEN (grimly): It had better come soon.

FIRST PATRIOT: We're waiting for Nulachucky Jack to get

here with his mountain men.

COLDEN (*looking offstage, right*): Land o' Joshua! Here come some more!

(JEB CRAWFORD *enters from stage right. He is helping a wounded soldier who has a leg wound. JEB, himself, has a bloody bandage tied around his head. ELIZABETH walks towards him to help.*)

JEB: Here, take care of him, woman. Got to get back to the crossing. (*Surprised*) Saints alive . . . Aunt Elizabeth! What—?

ELIZABETH: Jeb! Jeb Crawford! (*Anxiously*) Are . . . are you hurt, nephew?

JEB (*making light of it*): La, just a strip off'n my scalp, Aunt Elizabeth! Nothing to it!

(*She relieves him of the wounded soldier, JEB turns to go.*)

ELIZABETH: Wait, Jeb! Wait!

JEB (*urgently*): Auntie, I've got to get back to the crossing!

ELIZABETH: Jeb, have you . . . have you seen or heard aught of my eldest . . . Hugh?

(*As JEB helps her lower the SECOND PATRIOT to a bed of hay on the floor.*)

JEB: Can't say I have, Auntie. Not since the battle of Stone Ferry, leastways. (*Chuckles*) But I can tell you of those two little wildcats . . . those young 'uns of your'n.

ELIZABETH (*startled*): My young . . . ? Robbie and Andy? But . . . but they are at home!

JEB (*going off, still chuckling*): Reckon I know my own kin when I see 'em!

ELIZABETH: Jeb, where did you see them? Tell me!

JEB: Last time I saw them they were down in a meadow about a mile yonder, popping away at every Redcoat they could sight, and having the time of their young lives!

(*JEB exits as ELIZABETH stands mutely looking after him. The SECOND PATRIOT is looking at her with a thoughtful frown.*)

SECOND PATRIOT: If you please, ma'm . . .

ELIZABETH (*starts*): Oh, forgive me, lad. I'll attend you now.

(*She walks to him and kneels down by his side. He is propped on his elbow.*)

SECOND PATRIOT: Tain't that, ma'm. It's concerning your young 'uns . . .

ELIZABETH: Have you see them?

SECOND PATRIOT: Can't say for certain, ma'm, but . . . (*Hesitates.*)

ELIZABETH: But, what? Tell me!

SECOND PATRIOT: Is one of them a tall lad, with kinda red hair?

ELIZABETH: Aye, Robbie!

SECOND PATRIOT: And t'other a mite shorter . . . heavy set?

ELIZABETH: Aye, those are my boys!

COLDEN (*coming up*): Mrs. Jackson, will you . . .

SECOND PATRIOT: Aye, their name was Jackson, ma'm. And they were brothers I—

ELIZABETH (*agonized*): Were? You say . . . were? They are not . . . ?

SECOND PATRIOT (*hastily*): Nay, ma'm, I don't mean it that way.

ELIZABETH: Where did you see them? What happened to them?

SECOND PATRIOT: I'm afraid they got took . . . took by the Redcoats. (*Mumbles*) Sorry, ma'm.

ELIZABETH: Are you sure?

SECOND PATRIOT: Saw them taken off by a couple of Regulars. Would have tried to help them, but didn't have a grain of powder in my horn . . . an' got hit in the leg . . .

COLDEN: Your sons, Mrs. Jackson? (ELIZABETH *nods.*) Sorry to hear that.

ELIZABETH: Where do you think they will take them?

(COLDEN *is kneeling by the side of the soldier, examining his wound.*)

COLDEN: Bandages, Mrs. Jackson. (*She hands him some bandages.*) Like as not take them to Camden. Military prison there.

ELIZABETH (*horrified*): Camden . . . that horrible plague hole? Oh, no! . . . My poor lads . . . my poor, poor lads!

111

(*Pauses as she looks around at the wounded.*) Will you
. . . will you need me here much longer, Doctor Colden?
COLDEN (*looking about*): Matters seem to be well in hand,
and I should get more assistance soon. Why . . . surely
you are not thinking of seeking out your lads in Camden?
ELIZABETH: I must. When I think of the stories I've heard
about the fate of those poor lads held in the Camden
prison . . . and that my own dear boys . . .
COLDEN: But Camden is more than one hundred and fifty
miles away, woman!
ELIZABETH: If it were one thousand and fifty miles away,
Doctor Colden, I would find my way to their sides!
(COLDEN *looks up at her with admiration.*)
COLDEN (*murmurs*): Lord bless you, my dear.

SCENE 4

The headquarters of General LORD RAWDEN in Camden,
North Carolina. The room is simply furnished with a desk
and a few chairs. On the desk, stage right, are an inkpot,
quills, and some papers. A British flag hangs on the wall
behind the desk. Daylight enters from windows in the back
wall. It is morning, several days after the previous scene.

At curtain rise, RAWDEN is seated behind the desk checking some lists. His aide-de-camp, CAPTAIN FURNESS, enters
from stage right.

FURNESS: M'Lord General, there's a woman outside who
begs an audience with your lordship.
RAWDEN: What manner of woman, Captain Furness?
FURNESS: Indeed 'tis hard to say, m'lord. She's so be-spattered
with that cursèd red soil of this countryside, I would not
venture to judge her age or her station.
RAWDEN: What concern has she with me?
FURNESS: She would not say; except that she comes directly
from the rebel camp of Colonel Davie.
RAWDEN (*interested*): Ho, indeed! Show her in.
FURNESS (*bowing*): Aye, m'lord.

RAWDEN: Perhaps she has some information that will help us lay that scoundrel by the heels. (*He returns to his papers.*)
(FURNESS *exits stage right and addresses* ELIZABETH.)

FURNESS (*voice offstage*): Come in, madam. His lordship will see you.
(RAWDEN *rises as* ELIZABETH *enters followed by* FURNESS.)

ELIZABETH: General Rawden?

RAWDEN: Yes. (*Motions to chair*) Please be seated. (*After they both are seated*) Might I inquire your name, and the purpose of this visit?

ELIZABETH: Mrs. Elizabeth Jackson, sir.

RAWDEN: And what concern have you with me, Mrs. Jackson?

ELIZABETH: My two sons are being held here as prisoners of war. I beg of you—

RAWDEN (*interrupts her, lifting his hand*): My dear madam! If you have made this journey in some vain hope of effecting their release, then I'm sorry to inform you that your mission is indeed ill-advised.
(*His eyes turn to the list before him, scanning the names.*)

ELIZABETH: Sir, you must listen to me—

RAWDEN (*interrupting sharply*): If you please, my good woman! (*He studies the list for a moment. A frown forms on his face.*) Hmm . . . I presume these are the two rebels . . . Robert Jackson, age fifteen. Andrew Jackson, age . . . (*Incredulous*) By the saints . . . only thirteen years of age?

ELIZABETH: Aye, sir, my young ones . . . children . . . mere children!
(RAWDEN *is trying to fight down his humane feelings as he continues to refer to the paper.*)

RAWDEN: Taken at the engagement before Hanging Rock, while bearing arms. (*Looking up at* ELIZABETH, *angry because of his own conflict.*) Madam, if they were old enough to take up arms against His Majesty's troops, then, children or no, they are old enough to suffer the consequences for their acts against the Crown!

ELIZABETH: Sir, I have just come from the prison, where I was told that Andrew, my youngest, has suffered a wound, and—

RAWDEN (*softens*): Indeed, I am sorry, madam, truly sorry. But if I were to order their release, I would be lacking in duty to my king and country.

ELIZABETH: How can you talk of duty to me, their mother? If they were your own, sir . . .

RAWDEN (*looking at her speculatively*): Hmm . . . you love those sons of yours, don't you, madam?

ELIZABETH (*fervently*): Love them more than anything on God's earth!

RAWDEN: And you would do anything in your power to gain their release . . . ?

ELIZABETH: Aye, sir, anything.

RAWDEN: Very well, we shall see. Captain Furness!

FURNESS (*stepping forward*): Aye, m'lord?

(RAWDEN *opens his desk drawer, takes out a form.*)

RAWDEN: Write out a release for those two young rebels.

ELIZABETH: May heaven bless you, sir!

(FURNESS *is writing, leaning over the desk.*)

RAWDEN: Aye, madam, I will grant their release. But . . . (*Pauses.*)

ELIZABETH (*tightly*): But, what, sir?

RAWDEN: On the condition that you give me answer to three questions . . . honestly, and to the best of your knowledge.

ELIZABETH: And what, I pray you, are those questions?

RAWDEN: One, how many men are under the command of Colonel Davie? Two, what arms have they at their disposal? Three, by what means, and in what manner do they receive their supplies?

(ELIZABETH *rises from her chair, looks at him with contempt.*)

ELIZABETH: I see—you expect me to buy my sons' freedom with the lives and blood of my countrymen?

RAWDEN (*with a shrug*): Well, Mrs. Jackson, you say you love your sons . . .

ELIZABETH: Aye, I love my sons . . . love them too well to see the mother that bore them turn traitor to their country. Good day, sir! (*She turns and starts walking toward exit.*)

RAWDEN (*rises, calls out*): Mrs. Jackson!

ELIZABETH (*turning*): Aye?

RAWDEN: In truth, I did not expect you to answer my questions.

ELIZABETH (*scornfully*): Perchance then, it just amused an English *gentleman* to torture a woman?

RAWDEN (*stung, shouts*): No, by heaven! Do you think I have no feelings? (*Softer*) Why . . . why I have two young sons of my own back home in England. And if it were not for my duty . . . my duty to my king and country—

ELIZABETH: Duty! Duty to your king and country! What manner of king, what manner of country is yours, that demands that children be cast into a plague-infested prison to suffer a horrible, certain death? What will it serve you, your country, or your beloved king if my sons die? Will that, and only that, satisfy your precious sense of duty?

RAWDEN: May I remind you, madam, that you, too, show a sense of duty . . . duty to your *own* countrymen? Aye, for which you would e'en sacrifice your two sons, not to betray your own people.

ELIZABETH: Ours is an allegiance to a *cause*, not a king, sir! The cause of free men fighting for justice and liberty! And it is the best cause . . . a cause worth dying for. Were I to betray that cause, I would not betray a king, who is but a man. Nor would I betray a people or a country alone. I would betray humanity itself.

(RAWDEN *regards her with admiration and wonder.*)

RAWDEN: Hmmm . . . is that how all you Americans feel, madam?

ELIZABETH: All *liberty* loving Americans, sir!

RAWDEN (*soberly*): If that be so, then I would see this curséd struggle over with. Aye, and that today! For 'tis naught but a waste of precious English lives.

(*She comes forward to make a last desperate appeal.*)

ELIZABETH: I beg of you, sir . . . if you won't free my boys, at least give me the consolation of seeing them?

RAWDEN (*growls as he picks up the quill*): Won't be necessary.

ELIZABETH: You . . . you are going to sign . . . free them?

RAWDEN (*as he signs the order*): Yes, yes! Take your precious young rebels! Take them home! (*Stands up and points his quill at her.*) And for the sake of all that's holy, see if you can employ that irresistible eloquence of yours to keep them there. (*He picks up the order.*) Come along, now, I'll accompany you to the prison.

SCENE 5

A section in the Camden prison. A dim light enters from a single window left.

At curtain rise ANDY *and* ROBBIE *are seen lying on straw pallets covered with rough gunnysacks. A bucket and dipper stand on the floor near by.* ROBBIE *is lying on his side, his arm covering his face, his back turned to* ANDY. ANDY *is lying on his side, resting on his elbow, facing* ROBBIE.

ANDY: Robbie, why did they move us away from the other prisoners?

ROBBIE (*mumbles*): Dunno.

ANDY: You think maybe so we won't catch the plague? (ROBBIE *doesn't respond.*) You think that's it, Robbie?

ROBBIE (*half turning, crossly*): I be telling you I don't know!

(ANDY *moves his leg up and down, testing it.*)

ANDY: My leg feels right fit again, Robbie.

ROBBIE (*mumbles*): That's good.

ANDY: Aye, but what good are legs in this hole of a prison. Can't go nowhere. (*After a pause*) Lordy, Robbie, there was no sense in you being caught, too! You should have run for the woods.

ROBBIE (*angrily*): Told you a thousand times why! Must you keep talking about it?

ANDY: Because I think there were no sense to it, that's why! (*After a long sullen pause*) Robbie, when do you think they'll let us go?

ROBBIE: Dunno.

ANDY: Think we'll be here 'till (*Gulps at the thought*) 'till the war is over?

ROBBIE: P'haps.

ANDY: Robbie, reckon ma knows where we be?

ROBBIE. Maybe.

ANDY (*trying to arouse hope in* ROBBIE, *and himself*): I wager if she did know, she'd get us out, aye, Robbie? (ROBBIE *doesn't answer.*) You know ma. She'd ride like all get out into Camden . . . clear up to the British lines, and she'd—

ROBBIE (*with half a sob*): Andy, do hush that fool mouth of yours!

(ANDY *is taken aback by* ROBBIE's *harshness. He gets up and walks away with a slight limp. Then he comes back, looks down at* ROBBIE *anxiously, wondering. He kneels down by* ROBBIE's *side.*)

ANDY: You . . . you feeling bad, Robbie?

ROBBIE (*sorry for his crossness*): I . . . I reckon it . . . it's the heat bothering me, Andy.

ANDY (*surprised*): Heat? Lor-a-me, Robbie, it's chill enough in here to freeze a body's . . . . (*He stops as a horrible thought crosses his mind.*) Robbie, you haven't been took . . . took with the plague, have you? (*Urgently, as he gets no answer*) Robbie, have you?

ROBBIE (*turning his head*): No, no! I'm all right! Just let me be, will you!

ANDY: Let . . . let me feel your head, Robbie. That's what Ma does.

(ROBBIE *swings around and moves away quickly from* ANDY's *outstretched hand.*)

ROBBIE (*frantically*): No, stay away from me, I tell you!

ANDY (*now deeply concerned*): But, Robbie . . .

ROBBIE: Andy Jackson, you come an inch closer and I'll . . . I'll strike you down! You mind me now . . . (*Coughs*)

117

I'll strike you down! So help me heaven I will! (ANDY *stands up and moves back a step. He looks down at* ROBBIE *helplessly, as* ROBBIE *drops back to his pallet weakly, coughing. Then he seems to be sobbing, his arm flung over his face.*) Andy . . .

ANDY (*quickly*): Aye, Robbie?

ROBBIE: I'm . . . I'm powerful thirsty.

ANDY (*eager to do something for him*): I'll fetch you some water!

(*He hurries over to the bucket, dips up some water and comes back to kneel at* ROBBIE'S *side. As he holds the dipper to* ROBBIE'S *lips,* ELIZABETH *enters from the right. She takes a few steps toward her boys, then stops to look at them.* RAWDEN *enters, then stands some distance behind her.* ELIZABETH *is making an effort to compose herself.* ANDY, *after a while, looks up and sees her. The dipper falls from his hand, spattering* ROBBIE.)

ANDY (*low, unbelievingly*): Ma! . . . (*Louder*) Ma!

ROBBIE (*his eyes closed, weakly*): Andy, if you aren't the clumsiest—

ANDY (*rising and turning to* ROBBIE): It's ma, Robbie! Ma is here!

ROBBIE: Have you gone off'n your head?

(ROBBIE *turns and raises himself on his elbow, as* ANDY *rushes over to* ELIZABETH. ROBBIE *shakes his head. Then he stares at* ELIZABETH, *not quite believing it.* ANDY *is in* ELIZABETH'S *arms.* ANDY *releases her and they walk up to* ROBBIE *together.*)

ANDY (*brushing tears from his eyes*): I knew you'd come! Robbie, didn't I just say that ma would find us? Didn't I?

ROBBIE (*hardly more than a whisper*): Ma . . . it . . . is it really you?

(ELIZABETH *kneels by* ROBBIE'S *side, cradles his head against her bosom.*)

ELIZABETH: Aye, Robbie lad, it's me. It's your ma, come to take you home.

(*She presses her lips to his forehead, then places her palm on his brow, looks toward* RAWDEN. *There is* anxiety and pain in her eyes. RAWDEN, who has been standing at a distance taking in the scene, lifts his eyebrows inquiringly. ELIZABETH nods sadly. RAWDEN turns his eyes to the floor, shakes his head, with a mixed feeling of guilt and sympathy.)

ELIZABETH: You feeling poorly, Robbie?

ROBBIE: Mighty poorly, ma. I reckon maybe I've caught the plague.

ELIZABETH: Nonsense, lad. We'll get you home, and before long you'll be kicking up your heels like a colt in springtime.

(As ANDY moves closer, ELIZABETH motions him back.)

RAWDEN (walks up a few paces): I have placed a cart at your disposal, ma'm, and ordered it stocked with blankets and provisions to see you home.

ELIZABETH: You are very kind, sir.

(ANDY is looking at RAWDEN in cold hostility, as ELIZABETH helps ROBBIE to his feet.)

ROBBIE: Ma, then you . . . then you aren't angry at us for not minding you and . . . and running off to the war 'way we did?

ELIZABETH: Lad, there is no room in my heart for anger at this moment. (Looks at RAWDEN) nor a place in my heart for hate. (Smiling, in mock threat) But you two rascals . . . you just wait 'till I get you home!

ANDY: Ma, Robbie didn't need to be caught by the Redcoats. He could have got clean away if—

ROBBIE (interrupts, weakly): Oh, hush your mouth, Andy Jackson. If you aren't the talkinest mortal ever born . . .

(They start walking towards exit, ELIZABETH supporting ROBBIE, ANDY trailing behind. RAWDEN comes forward, tries to take ROBBIE's other arm, but ROBBIE shrinks away from RAWDEN's hand and looks at him coldly.)

ELIZABETH (with mild reproof): Robbie . . .

(RAWDEN is not offended. He does not withdraw his hand. Smiles, with kindly understanding.)

RAWDEN: Oh, come ye now, lad . . . this may be your only chance to get this close to a Redcoat . . . (Afterthought) I hope.

(ROBBIE *looks down at the proffered hand, accepts his help. They continue walking toward exit,* ANDY *straggling far behind.*)

ELIZABETH: I shall return the cart you so kindly provided, sir.

RAWDEN: Not at all, ma'm. No need to do so, I assure you.

ELIZABETH: I mean to return *with* it, sir.

RAWDEN: Return *with* it? I don't understand.

ELIZABETH: Aye, as soon as my boys are home, and need me no longer, I shall return to care for the other mothers' sons imprisoned here, who must be in sore need of care and nursing. That is, with your permission, sir.

RAWDEN: Ma'm, you have my permission. And, may I add, my deepest respect and admiration.

(*When* ELIZABETH, ROBBIE *and* RAWDEN *exit,* ANDY *stops and turns. With a dark scowl he places his two fists on his hips and takes a last look at their prison. Then, with narrowed eyes and jutting jaw, he walks up to the bucket and kicks it smartly across the floor with his wounded leg. He gasps, grasps his leg and dances around in pain.*)

ANDY (*gritting his teeth*): Dad-blast those murdering Redcoats!

ELIZABETH (*voice offstage*): Andy!

ANDY (*hobbling towards exit*): Aye, ma . . . I'm coming, I'm coming!

CURTAIN

The Spy

By HENRY H. WALSH

As adapted from *The Spy*
by James Fenimore Cooper

THE SPY

CHARACTERS: 15 males; 2 females;
any number of male extras at will to
serve as spectators at the
court-martial

PLAYING TIME: 60 minutes

SETS: Two

~§ Historical Notes

Honor and fame came quickly to James Fenimore Cooper immediately after the publication of *The Spy* in the year 1822. The novel was an instant success, enthusiastically received in America and England, and brought him recognition and popularity which he continued to hold for more than a century. However, what attention he commands today depends not as much on his merit as a writer as it does on the significant place he holds in the literary, social and political history of our nation.

Cooper began writing at a time when the literary dependence of America was on English authorship, and it was still currently believed that if one wished to achieve literary fame he must draw his scenes from English lands and dress his characters in English garb. It was only after the War of 1812 that the nation began feeling a sense of self. The struggle for political independence and survival was over, but the struggle to throw off subservience to European culture and establish one distinctly American in character had just begun. Cooper's books fitted into the American landscape to perfection, for they were American to the core.

Flashing before our eyes are his Indians, pioneers, hunters, planters, trappers, mountains and plains, lakes and oceans: splashed on a huge canvas with bold strokes of vivid primary colors. One has to step back from the canvas to appreciate the large effects of his wide brush strokes.

Ralph Waldo Emerson, in 1837, with his hand on the pulse of our people, expressed it well: "Our day of dependence, our long apprenticeship to the learnings of other lands, draws to a close. The Millions that around us are rushing into life cannot always be fed on the mere remains of foreign harvests. Events, actions arise, that must be sung, and will sing themselves."

James Fenimore Cooper was one of the first to sing the song of America. And there lay the secret of his success.

❧ Production Notes

⟨ Characters

MR. WHARTON, *father of Sally, Franny and Henry Wharton*
CAESAR, *the Wharton house slave*
FRANNY, *Mr. Wharton's younger daughter*
SALLY, *Mr. Wharton's elder daughter*
GEORGE WASHINGTON, *traveling incognito as John Harper*
HENRY WHARTON, *captain in the British army, Mr. Wharton's son*
MAJOR PEYTON DUNWOODIE, *officer in the American army*
CAPTAIN LAWTON, *officer in the American army*
SERGEANT, *in the American army*
HARVEY BIRCH, *the spy, a neighbor of the Whartons*
FIRST AMERICAN SOLDIER
SECOND AMERICAN SOLDIER
THIRD AMERICAN SOLDIER
CLERK, *of the court, sergeant in rank*
COLONEL SINGLETON, *senior judge of the court*
MAJOR PENDLETON, *second judge of the court*
CAPTAIN RICHARDSON, *third judge of the court*
SPECTATORS, *in the courtroom*
(If production and casting problems require more economy, the trial may be staged as a closed proceeding without spectators.)

⟨ Scenes

SCENE 1: The Wharton country home in White Plains, N.Y., on an evening in October, 1780.
SCENE 2: The same as SCENE 1, on the following morning.

Scene 3: The living room in a manor house, set up to conduct a court-martial, two days later.

((Settings

Scene 1: The living room in an upperclass country home of the American Colonial period. Scene 2: the same. Scene 3: A large room in a country manor house of the American Colonial period.

((Costumes

American Colonial civilian and military dress. Mr. Wharton in Scene 1 is dressed as a wealthy, upperclass American Colonial. In Scene 2 he wears a long traveling cape over his other garments. In place of his silver-buckled shoes he wears leather boots. He holds a tricornered hat in his hand. Franny Wharton is simply gowned in the long-skirted, half-sleeved dress of the period. In Scene 2 she wears the same, but has added a fine lace apron over her dress. In Scene 3 she wears a pelisse with the hood thrown back. Sally Wharton is dressed similarly to her sister. Caesar, being a privileged house slave, is costumed in the same manner as his master, but his clothing is conservative in color and devoid of braiding and other ornamentation. Washington (as Harper) in Scene 1 appears in civilian clothing of velvet or wool, conservatively dark in color. His breeches are tucked into high riding boots. A neck-cloth is tied around his throat. He carries a tricornered hat in his hand. In Scene 3 he appears at the court-martial in full military uniform: blue coat with gold epaulets, buff breeches, and high boots. He carries a sword at his side and a tricornered hat in his hand. He could be wearing a white wig. Henry Wharton in Scene 1 enters wearing the rough homespun outfit of a commoner. A dangling neck-cloth is tied around his throat. He is disguised with a red wig on his head and a black patch over one eye. A shabby cloak is thrown over his shoulders. He carries a tricornered hat in his hand. In SCENE 2 he appears in rich, colorful clothing. In SCENE 3 he wears the same costume as in SCENE 2. Peyton Dunwoodie is in the uniform of the American army officer: blue coat with buff trimmings, buff breeches, high riding boots, and sword. The three soldiers, the sergeant, and the clerk of the court are in uniforms of the Continental Army. Harvey Birch is disguised as a Protestant clergyman: black frock coat and dark breeches, waistcoat, stock, stockings and buckle-shoes. He wears a clergyman's collar. Colonel Singleton, Major Pendleton and Captain Richardson are in the uniforms of officers in the American army. They carry swords at their sides. The Spectators are in civilian or military dress.

❲ Properties

In SCENES 1 and 2, living room furniture of the period: chairs, sideboard, wine decanter and glasses on a silver salver, silver candlesticks, rugs, fireplace tools, paintings and portraits, 2 embroidery frames and sewing baskets, newspaper (tabloid size), red electric bulb to simulate glow of fire in fireplace. SCENE 3: a Bible, a thirteen-starred American flag, papers, inkpot and quills, small knife, Henry Wharton's articles of disguise.

❲ Lighting

SCENE 1: Candlelight and fireplace glow. SCENE 2: Bright morning daylight streaming in through windows. SCENE 3: Daylight.

Scene III - "The Spy"

127

The Spy

SCENE 1

The living room in the Wharton home in Westchester County, N.Y. on a rainy, blustery evening in October, 1780. It is a moderate sized room, simply furnished, but containing unmistakable signs of wealth and good taste: the highly polished richness of the furniture; the rugs on the floor; the silver candlesticks; the gold framed portraits and paintings on the walls, etc. Two deeply recessed windows with tie-back drapes form alcoves in the back wall. To the left, a fireplace, casting a red glow into the room. A door, right, leads to other sections of the house. The room is lighted by several branched candlesticks.

At curtain rise MR. WHARTON is seated center front, facing the fireplace. He is reading Rivington's Loyal Gazette, a two-page newspaper the size of a modern tabloid which was published in New York City before, and during, the British occupation of the town. FRANNY and SALLY WHARTON are seated left of the fireplace, with FRANNY to the left of SALLY. Both are working on embroidery frames by the light of a candlestick resting on a table between them. CAESAR enters and begins to close the window drapes.

CAESAR: Mm-mm! Just listen to that rain! Comin' down fit to drown the whole world. (Grins) And us without an ark between us and Kingdom Come.

FRANNY (turning her head to look at him with a smile): Do you think it will rain for forty days and forty nights, Caesar?

CAESAR: Sure 'pears like it, don't it, Miss Franny?

FRANNY: But isn't it always so in late October, Caesar? Once

128

it starts to rain it just forgets to stop.

(CAESAR *is standing before a sideboard between the two windows, placing a decanter of wine and a wineglass on a silver salver. He carries it to* MR. WHARTON'S *end table.*)

CAESAR: Ain't it the truth, Miss Franny?

WHARTON (*his eyes still on the paper; sighs sadly*): Very much like this horrible war, I'm afraid. It, too, seems to go on, and on, and on, as if it never means to stop until the land is drenched with blood, and there isn't a single reb . . . (*He stops, throws a quick glance at* FRANNY.) . . . American soldier left alive. (*To* CAESAR, *who is pouring the wine*) Thank you, Caesar. (CAESAR *bows.*) Five years . . . five years of bloody struggle, and no end in sight.

SALLY: I see General Gage has suffered a severe defeat in the south at the hands of Lord Cornwallis, father.

FRANNY (*with a toss of her head and a scornful sniff*): And where did you hear that, sister?

SALLY (*indicating Gazette*): Printed there . . . in the Rivington Loyal Gazette.

FRANNY: You mean the Rivington *Lying* Gazette, don't you?

WHARTON (*exchanging smiles with* SALLY): I take it, my little rebel . . .

FRANNY: *Patriot!*

WHARTON (*hangs his head in mock contrition*): Forgive me, dear child, I stand corrected. (*Looks up at her with a smile*) Patriot. (*Points to top of Gazette*) I was about to remark that you evidently don't believe what is stated here under the masthead of the Gazette . . . (*Reads*) "The ever open and uninfluenced press, fronting on the corner of Queen Street, in the City of New York."

FRANNY: Hah! False on both counts! It is no longer named Queen Street. It is now *Pearl* Street. And . . . uninfluenced? I say, poppycock! Everyone knows that James Rivington is but a creature in the pay of the British command, and that his paper is subsidized by the British and the Tories to spread lies throughout the Colonies to dishearten the

Americans and have them lay down their arms! In truth, father, if one were to believe what is printed in that paper, then more Americans are killed in battle every week than there are white inhabitants in the entire country!

WHARTON (*hiding a smile behind the paper as he looks at it*): Now that you mention it, Franny, it does state here that . . . "The rebels . . ." (*Looks up quickly over the top of the paper*) I but merely quote from the paper, child!

FRANNY: Hum!

WHARTON (*looking at paper, reads*): ". . . in their retreat after their engagement with Lord Cornwallis's regulars, left thousands dead on the field of battle."

FRANNY (*triumphant*): Hah! And how many times have they reported the death of General Washington?

WHARTON (*scratching his ear with a wry smile, he turns back to the paper and reads*): ". . . and from most reliable sources, it is reported that General Washington has not been seen for several days, and it is said he has been slain and secretly buried . . ."

FRANNY (*again triumphant*): Hah! It is indeed fortunate for the American cause that General Washington has more lives than a cat. Oh, if we only could get the Pennsylvania Journal, or any other news gazette that favors the cause of the patriots!

SALLY (*scornfully*): Patriots! In my judgment, dear sister mine, a patriot means one thing—and only one thing: he who is loyal to our sovereign, King George the Third.

FRANNY (*bridling*): Sally Wharton, if you for one moment believe that I will sit here and suffer in silence . . .

WHARTON (*disturbed, rises and walks to fireplace as he talks*): Now, now, children, I pray you, let us not carry this bitter war into our home and destroy such measure of peace as is afforded us here. We *must* try to remain neutral in this struggle.

SALLY: Neutral? 'Tis easy to say, father, but quite difficult to *feel* neutral when you consider that your son, Henry— our brother, whom we all love so dearly, is an officer in his majesty's army, and at this very moment may be engaged in mortal combat with a rebel force! (*She sees* FRANNY's *back up again, but is unrelenting.*) Excuse me, sister. *Continental* force, then. (*Snaps*) I hope that will do. (FRANNY *looks at her coldly for a moment, then rises and starts to leave the room.* SALLY *catches her hand and stops her, contritely.*) I'm sorry. Truly I am, dear Franny. I just keep forgetting that you are betrothed to Peyton Dunwoodie, and . . .

FRANNY (*snatching her hand away angrily*): Major Peyton Dunwoodie! Who is, I'm proud to say, an officer on General Washington's staff!

WHARTON (*trying to restore peace*): Now, Franny child, please!

FRANNY: And if you think I feel the way I do only because I am betrothed to Peyton, then you couldn't be more mistaken! For I firmly believe in the justice of the American cause, and, if I were a man, would gladly lay down my life for it!

SALLY (*mockingly, low, as she silently applauds*): Hear! Hear!

WHARTON (*sharp reprimand*): Sally, stop deliberately provoking your sister! She has a perfect right to follow the dictates of her conscience . . . even though we may not be in agreement with her on this matter.

SALLY: And Henry, father, has he not also the right to follow the dictates of his conscience, by holding fast in his loyalty to the crown?

WHARTON: You know I respect him for it.

SALLY: And you, Franny? Do you respect your brother the less for remaining true to his sovereign?

FRANNY (*restrained*): I love him no less than you do, Sally. And as for "remaining true to his sovereign," as you put it, Henry was an officer in the British army long before our separation from England. He could not have done less than accompany his regiment to New York when it was brought here from England.

WHARTON (*sighs*): Ah, me, how sad it is to find Henry and Peyton on opposite sides in this conflict. They were such good friends, inseparable companions from childhood on. And now . . . (*He shakes his head sadly, then turns to* FRANNY *with a frown.*) Nevertheless, I implore you, Franny, do be careful how you talk, for we find ourselves in a most awkward position here. Indeed, most awkward, to say the least. To the south, the British forces hardly more than twenty miles away. And to the north, the American encampment. And here we are . . . caught right in the middle of it all.

SALLY: We should have remained in New York.

FRANNY: And continued to live under British occupation?

SALLY: Far better than living here under the constant threat of being turned out of our house for being loyal to the king.

WHARTON (*longingly*): And we could have the pleasure of seeing Henry, if we were in New York. It is almost a year . . .

FRANNY: Is he still stationed there?

WHARTON: Aye, and very well thought of by Sir Henry Clinton, I hear.

FRANNY (*puzzled*): How do you know this?

WHARTON: From our neighbor, Harvey Birch.

FRANNY: Harvey Birch? Really, father! That contemptible creature! He's known to be a spy for the British!

WHARTON: Pshaw, a mere rumor, I say!

FRANNY: Rumor? How can you explain the ease with which he comes and goes through the British lines, pretending to be a peddler? Only one in the pay of the British . . .

CAESAR (*coming in, apprehensively*): Someone at the back door, Massa Wharton.

SALLY: Who would be abroad on a night like this?

WHARTON (*mutters*): 'Tis best you look through the peep-hole first, Caesar. One can't be too cautious these days.

CAESAR: I did, Massa Wharton. Look like lone traveler a-saddle.

WHARTON: Are you sure he's alone?

CAESAR: 'Pears to be, Massa Wharton.

WHARTON: Then open the door and have him in.

CAESAR (*as he leaves*): Whoever it be, goin' to be mighty wet. Rain comin' down like old debbil.

SALLY (*anxiously*): Do you think you should?

WHARTON: How can we turn anyone away from our door, Sally?

SALLY: But in these times . . . with bushwhackers roaming the countryside . . . ?

CAESAR (*voice offstage*): Come in, sir. Ol' Caesar he bid you welcome.

HARPER (*voice offstage*): Thank you, Caesar. Will you ask your master if he could accommodate me for the night?

CAESAR (*comes in, whispers to* WHARTON): A gen'lman, sir.

WHARTON (*low*): Are you certain, Caesar?

CAESAR (*with a smile*): Ever know ol' Caesar to make mistake, Massa Wharton? (*Chuckles*) Not *that* kind of mistake, leastways.

WHARTON (*smiles*): No, I guess not. (*Walks to door*) Do come in, sir.

GEORGE WASHINGTON, *traveling incognito as* MR. HARPER, *walks in.*)

HARPER (*bowing*): Mr. Wharton?

WHARTON: Aye, sir. Take the gentleman's cloak, Caesar, and hang it by the chimney to dry. (CAESAR *takes* HARPER's *cloak.*)

HARPER: You are most kind, sir.

WHARTON: Not at all, sir. (*Introduction*) My two daughters, sir. Sally . . . and Frances.

HARPER (*bowing*): A great pleasure, young ladies.

SALLY: Welcome to The Locusts, sir.

FRANNY: Welcome, indeed, sir.

HARPER: I hope I am not inconveniencing your household. (CAESAR *has walked to the sideboard to fetch another wine glass.*)

WHARTON: Not at all, sir. Not at all. May I apologize for not giving you more immediate entry? These are troublesome times. Most troublesome times.

HARPER: Indeed, I understand. Only a rash soul would leave his latchstrings hanging out these days. (*Short laugh*)

133

Truth to tell, I was refused shelter by your neighbor.

WHARTON: Oh?

FRANNY: Indeed, sir?

HARPER: The most she would do for me was to direct me to your door.

WHARTON: Aye, that would be Kate, Harvey Birch's housekeeper. Perhaps if Harvey himself were at home . . .

HARPER (*slight start*): Harvey Birch? Was that the home of Harvey Birch?

WHARTON: Yes. Do you know him?

HARPER: Why . . . (*Hesitant*) I believe I have heard his name mentioned.

FRANNY (*grimly*): Indeed you very well may have. He's . . .

WHARTON (*stops her; mild reproof*): Franny, if you please, dear. Harvey is our neighbor. (*To* HARPER) Come, sit down here by the fire, sir. (CAESAR *has poured the wine. He walks toward* HARPER *with a glass on a tray, as* HARPER *is seated.*) A glass of Madeira?

HARPER: You are most kind. Thank you. (CAESAR *hands* HARPER *the glass with a bow.*)

WHARTON (*lifting his glass*): And, to whose health have I the honor of drinking, sir?

HARPER: Ah, Harper. John Harper, sir.

WHARTON (*lifting his glass with formal precision*): Mr. Harper, I have the honor to drink to your health, and to hope you will sustain no injury from the rain to which you have been exposed.

(*The sisters occupy themselves again with their needlework, occasionally casting a covert, but admiring, glance at* HARPER.)

HARPER (*bowing*): Your health, sir.

(*They sip their wine.* WHARTON *extends a tobacco jar to* HARPER.)

WHARTON: A pipeful, Mr. Harper?

HARPER: No, thank you, Mr. Wharton. (*Extends his hand for jar.*) But if I may examine the quality of your tobacco? I account myself rather a connoisseur of the weed. (*He takes a pinch and puts it on his tongue.*)

WHARTON: I'm afraid it is not of the highest quality.

HARPER: It is not Virginian.

WHARTON (*fishing*): Ah, you are from Virginia, sir?

HARPER: I have spent considerable time in that colony.

WHARTON: Ah. (*Sighs*) I find it very difficult to get the quality of tobacco to which I have been accustomed.

HARPER: I should think the shops in New York might furnish the best in the country.

(*HARPER gazes at him steadily. As their eyes meet WHARTON drops his in some confusion.*)

WHARTON: Why, yes . . . there must be plenty in town, but the war has made communication with the city too dangerous to be risked for so trifling an article as tobacco.

(*HARPER nods, remains silent. WHARTON tries a new tack to feel him out.*)

WHARTON (*with more vigor than necessary*): I wish from the bottom of my heart this unnatural struggle were over, that we could return to New York and meet our friends and relatives again.

HARPER: It is much to be desired by everyone, I'm sure.

WHARTON: Have you heard if there have been any movements of any consequences since the French our . . . ah, allies, have arrived?

HARPER: No news has yet reached the public, I believe.

WHARTON: Is it thought that any important steps will be taken?

HARPER (*looks up from the fire with a slightly amused smile*): Is it intimated that there are some in the offing, sir?

WHARTON (*quickly*): Oh, nothing in particular, but it is natural to expect some new action from the arrival of so powerful a force under Rochambeau. (*HARPER nods his head but makes no reply.*) There appears to be more activity in the south. General Gates and Lord Cornwallis, the British commander, seem prepared to bring the war to an issue there.

SALLY (*crowing*): Much to the misfortune of Gates, we understand.

FRANNY (*tartly*): That remains to be seen, sister mine! (*As

HARPER *looks up at her with a soft, paternal smile,* FRANNY *feels that she has been uncautious and stammers.)* Mmmm . . . my sister and I sometimes differ in our opinions of the British.

HARPER (*with a broad smile*): On what particular points do you differ, may I inquire?

FRANNY: Sally thinks the British can never be beaten.

HARPER: Ah . . . and you, dear child?

FRANNY: I . . . I do not put so much faith in their invincibility.

HARPER (*smiles at her, turns to* SALLY): You doubtless find your present situation in the country tiresome, after being accustomed to the gaieties of the city, I should think?

SALLY: Excessively so! I do wish this war were over, that we might return to our friends once more.

HARPER: And you, Miss Frances . . . do you long as ardently for peace as your sister?

FRANNY (*looking down*): On many accounts, I certainly do. (*Steals a glance at* HARPER) But not at the expense of my countrymen's rights.

SALLY (*sharply*): Rights? Whose rights can be stronger than those of a sovereign? And what duty is clearer than to obey those who have a natural right to command?

> (WHARTON *is alarmed at* SALLY's *outburst. He eyes his guest apprehensively.* FRANNY *notes it, tries to ease the situation with a laugh, as she takes her sister's hand affectionately.*)

FRANNY: Did I not give you to understand that my sister and I differ in our political opinions? But we do have an impartial umpire in our father, who loves his own countrymen, and loves the British as well. So, he takes sides with neither, sir.

WHARTON (*quickly*): Yes, yes, I have friends in both armies.

HARPER (*turning to* WHARTON *with an amused smile*): And you, sir . . . how do you feel about each army?

WHARTON (*flounders, uncertain*): Why . . . why . . . his majesty's army . . . (HARPER *hides a smile at* WHARTON's *confusion.*) I mean . . . the British army has more experienced troops than the Continentals. But . . . but the Americans have met with distinguished success at times, I must say. Don't you . . .? (WHARTON *stops with great relief as* CAESAR *appears at the door.*) Yes, Caesar, what is it?

CAESAR (*glumly*): Another traveler . . . at the back door, Massa Wharton.

WHARTON: A gentleman, Caesar?

CAESAR (*with an emphatic shake of his head*): Uh-uh! Don't look like gen'lman to ol' Caesar! No, sir! Rough looking, redheaded man with black patch over eye.

WHARTON (*grudgingly*): Hmm . . . Well, we can't turn anyone away from our door. See that he is given food and accommodations. (*Afterthought*) In the servant quarters, Caesar.

CAESAR: Yes, Massa Wharton, I'll . . .

(HENRY WHARTON *enters in disguise. He walks quickly into the room in eager anticipation, but stops when he sees* HARPER. *He controls himself, steps forward boldly, acting the boor.*)

HENRY (*loud, overly hearty*): Ah, good evening! Good evening, gentlemen! (*Bows in the direction of his sisters.*) Ladies, your servant.

(*The sisters rise in dismay.* WHARTON *is frowning with annoyance, as* HARPER *regards* HENRY *closely.*)

CAESAR (*mutters*): He sure don't wait to be invited in, do he?

WHARTON (*stiffly*): Good evening, sir. My servant will look to your comfort, if you will be pleased to follow him.

CAESAR (*moving towards door*): This way, sir.

HENRY *is enjoying his play-acting. He ignores* WHARTON's *hint, walks to the fire and extends his hands to the warmth.*)

HENRY: Ah, this is pleasant! Very pleasant indeed! A cheerful fire, and . . . (*His eyes fasten on wine decanter*) By my soul, sir . . . (*Points to decanter*) I'll wager a gold guinea to a tuppence it's Madeira (WHARTON *watches him in stony silence, the sisters in open-mouthed disbelief, as he rushes over to the decanter, lifts the stopper and sniffs the* wine, *then turns to* WHARTON *with a chuckle.*) How right I was sir! (*He pours himself some wine in* WHARTON's *glass.*) By your leave, sir. (HARPER *has been regarding* HENRY *with a slight smile on his face.*)

WHARTON (*scowling*): Do help yourself.

HENRY (*lifting his glass*): Thankee, sir! Thankee! Your health, sir! (*He sips the wine, smacks his lips.*) Excellent! Excellent Madeira, I must say!

WHARTON (*drily*): I'm glad you appreciate my wine, sir.

HENRY: I do indeed. (*Lifts his glass again.*) To our better acquaintance, Mr. Wharton. (*Looking at* HARPER *narrowly*) And to you, sir . . . I don't believe I know your name.

HARPER (*with a slight bow*): John Harper.

HENRY (*intently*): Your face, Mr. Harper, seems familiar.

HARPER: I don't believe we have ever met, sir.

HENRY (*suspiciously*): No? But the way you scrutinize my person, Mr. Harper, would seem to indicate otherwise.

HARPER: Forgive me if I appear rude, sir. But, I was only thinking . . . (*Stops.*)

HENRY (*demands*): Aye, you were thinking what, sir?

HARPER (*amused*): . . . thinking how much more becoming you look in your British regimentals, Captain Wharton.

(HENRY, *his eyes remaining on* HARPER's *face, slowly lowers the glass to the table. The* WHARTONS *are struck speechless for a moment as they stare at* HENRY. *Then they begin to converge on him from all sides.*)

WHARTON: Henry! Henry! my son!

FRANNY: Yes, yes, it is Henry!

SALLY (*chuckling*): Oh, no! If this isn't just like that idiot brother of ours.

CAESAR (*popeyed*): Massa Henry!

(*The sisters are embracing him.* WHARTON *is holding his hands.*)

WHARTON (*overcome with emotion*): My son, my dear son . . .

HENRY: Father! . . Franny, my love! And Sally . . . my little Sally . . .

(*Suddenly, they all remember* HARPER's *presence, turn
their eyes towards him with varied expressions of worry,
wonderment, appeal, and suspicion.*)

CAESAR (*with a chuckle, but almost in tears as he holds one
of* HENRY's *hands in both of his*): Massa Henry, you sure
fooled all'n us, you did. Yes, sir!

HENRY (*narrowly*): Yes, all but this gentleman here.

SALLY (*as she lifts off his wig*): Please let us get rid of this
ridiculous wig!

FRANNY (*as she removes his patch*): And this patch.

HENRY (*who hasn't taken his eyes off* HARPER): Mr.
Harper . . .

HARPER: Aye Captain Wharton?

HENRY (*picking up his wineglass and taking a sip*): You say
we have never met before?

HARPER: No, I don't believe we ever have.

HENRY: Then, I must confess, I am at a loss to understand
how you recognized me.

HARPER (*with a smile*): As one enters the foyer directly at
the head of the stairway, there's a portrait . . .

HENRY (*looks at* HARPER *admiringly, laughs*): By heavens,
yes! Painted in my full regimentals in England. Hmm . . .
you must be a close observer, sir.

HARPER: Necessity has made me so. But, I must say, young
sir, you have embarked on a most dangerous escapade.
The American lines completely surround this sector.

HENRY (*curtly*): I was aware of the danger.

HARPER: But a British officer, coming in disguise, might be
hanged as a spy . . . if captured.

HENRY: I won't be taken.

HARPER (*soberly*): You may, young sir, you may.

FRANCES (*alarmed*): Oh, Henry . . . perhaps you shouldn't
have . . .

HENRY: Oh, fiddlesticks, Franny! (*Turns his eyes coldly on*
HARPER) Unless . . . (*Stops*)

HARPER (*with great dignity*): If you are concerned that I
might betray you, sir, I assure you, you need have no appre-
hensions on that score. It would indeed be poor return for

the gracious hospitality shown me by your father. And now, Mr. Wharton, if you will permit me to retire, I have had a wearisome day in the saddle.

WHARTON: Certainly, my good sir. Caesar, conduct Mr. Harper to the south chamber and see to his comfort.

CAESAR: Yes, Massa Wharton. (*Walks toward door*) Be pleased to follow me, sir.

HARPER: But, before I leave you, Captain Wharton . . .

HENRY: Aye, sir?

HARPER: This . . . this rash venture of yours, innocent as it may be, could result in dire consequences to yourself. If it does, I may have it in my power to help you. Bear that in mind, young sir. (HARPER *bows to the* WHARTONS *and exits, as the scene ends.*)

S C E N E 2

The same as Scene 1, the morning of the following day. The drapes are closed. MR. HARPER's *cloak is gone from the peg near the fireplace.* HENRY's *shabby cloak hangs there instead. His hat, wig and black patch rest on a chair.* CAESAR *enters, walks to the first window to tie back the drapes, and, as he does so, bright morning sunlight streams into the room. As he goes to the second window, MR.* WHARTON *enters and walks to the first window to look out.*

WHARTON: What a beautiful morning!

CAESAR: Yes sir, 'deed it is. (*Chuckles*) We don't need that ol' ark after all, Massa Wharton. Rain finally stopped.

(HENRY *enters the room with* FRANNY *trailing behind him, laughing gaily at some remark he has made.* HENRY *is richly dressed in one of his own civilian coats, looking bright and resplendent in contrast to his disheveled appearance of the previous evening.* CAESAR *and* WHARTON *beam at him affectionately.*)

FRANNY (*laughing*): Henry, I don't believe a word of it! I think you made it all up.

HENRY (*laughing*): 'Pon my honor, Franny, it *did* happen, and exactly in the manner I told you.

WHARTON: Have a good breakfast, Henry?

HENRY: By my faith, father, I haven't enjoyed a breakfast like that in ages!

WHARTON (*sighs*): How wonderful it would be to have you with us always. If only this beastly war . . . (*Shakes his head sadly.*)

HENRY: Never you fear, father, it will be over very soon. Those blasted rebels are beaten, but too pigheaded to know it. (FRANNY *is about to retort, but controls herself*) By the by, where is our good Mr. Harper . . . still a-bed?

WHARTON: He's gone, son. Rode off at break of dawn.

HENRY: Can't say I'm sorry to see him leave. There's something about that gentleman which bothers me no end. I don't know what it is . . .

WHARTON (*uneasily*): Do . . . do you think we have anything to fear? That he might . . . ?

FRANNY (*firmly*): I'll wager my very soul that we can trust his word, father!

  (CAESAR, *unobserved by all, nods his head in definite agreement.*)

HENRY (*skeptical*): And what makes you so sure of that, lovey?

FRANNY (*with knitted brow, groping for words*): Why . . . why . . . I don't know. It . . . It's just his manner . . . his whole being. Yes, there's something about him that's noble . . . great. It . . . it's hard to explain, but I know it. I can *feel* it.

  (CAESAR *exits, smiling at* FRANNY *and nodding his agreement.*)

HENRY: Appearances, my sweet, are but too often deceiving.

WHARTON (*anxiously*): When do you think you will make your way back to your lines, Henry? Tonight, perhaps?

HENRY (*throwing his arm around* FRANNY'S *waist and hugging her with a laugh*): Come, come, father, would you have me leave such lovely company so soon?

WHARTON: But the Continentals may be on the move again.

141

They may come upon you.

HENRY (*contemptuously*): Bah, a few guineas will buy off those rascals.

FRANNY (*quietly, controlling herself*): It couldn't buy off Major André, brother.

HENRY (*angrily*): Franny, I would rather you didn't mention that dastardly crime in my presence.

FRANNY (*showing some spirit*): Crime? He was a spy! A British spy!

HENRY: He was serving his king! The usages of war justified his conduct!

FRANNY: Then the usages of war justified his hanging!

WHARTON (*trying desperately to restore peace*): Oh, children! My dear children, don't . . .

HENRY (*bitterly*): Frances, you shock me! Indeed you do!

FRANNY (*placing her hand on his arm*): Henry, I . . .

HENRY: I suppose if I were to fall into the hands of the rebels, you would exult at my execution!

WHARTON (*sharply*): Henry!

FRANNY (*deeply hurt*): Henry! How . . . how can you say that! (*almost in tears*) You . . . you little know my heart.

WHARTON (*placing his hand on her head*): Frances, dear child, don't take seriously his hasty words.

HENRY (*very contrite, takes her hand*): Forgive me, my little sister. I suppose it is but natural for you to see the war through the eyes of Peyton Dunwoodie.

FRANNY (*wearily*): Oh, heavens above, Henry . . . (*She doesn't go on, turns away.*)

WHARTON: Henry, don't you think you ought to leave tonight?

HENRY: I can't leave until tomorrow evening, father. I have so arranged matters with Harvey Birch.

WHARTON (*alarmed*): Harvey Birch? What has he to do with it?

HENRY: It was he who lead me through the rebel lines. I must depend upon his guidance to lead me back to my regiment. (FRANNY *is regarding* HENRY *through cold, narrowed eyes.*)

142

WHARTON: Then Harvey Birch came here with you?

HENRY: Aye.

FRANNY: Where did you meet him?

HENRY: In the camp of Sir Henry Clinton, my commander.

FRANNY: Indeed? Is he then known to Clinton?

HENRY (*drily*): He certainly ought to be.

FRANNY: Then it *is* true! He *is* a British spy! How contemptible!

WHARTON: Don't hold him in contempt for loving his king.

HENRY (*disdainfully*): I'm afraid with Harvey Birch love of money is a stronger passion than love of king. (*Puzzled*) But why and how the rebels . . .

CAESAR (*offstage and coming up quickly, alarmed*): Massa Henry! Massa Henry! (CAESAR *enters.*) Massa Henry, run! Run for your horse!

HENRY: What is it, Caesar?

SALLY (*entering quickly*): A troop of rebel horses coming up the road, Henry!

WHARTON (*groans*): Oh, heaven preserve us!

FRANNY (*frantic*): Don't stand there like a clod! The back door!

HENRY (*with cold calmness*): Run? No, running is not my trade. Here I stay.

(SALLY *is peering out of the window.*)

WHARTON: But, my son . . .!

FRANNY: Don't be a fool, Henry! Hide!

WHARTON: At least put on your disguise!

(WHARTON *rushes over to* HENRY's *wig and eye patch, as* CAESAR *runs for his cloak.* WHARTON *clamps the wig on* HENRY's *head, very much askew, showing his black hair.* CAESAR *throws the cloak over his shoulder, as* WHARTON *hands* HENRY *his eye patch.*)

CAESAR: Your cloak, Massa Henry!

WHARTON: Put on that patch!

HENRY (*grudgingly*): Oh, very well, if you insist.

SALLY (*at the window, with great relief*): It's Peyton! Peyton Dunwoodie, at the head of a troop!

FRANNY (*running to the window*): Are you sure, Sally? (*She*

143

looks out.) Yes, it is Peyton!

HENRY (*scowling*): I can't see that it alters the situation any.

FRANNY: They are stopping before the door and dismount-
ing!

(*As everyone waits in anxious expectation amid tense
silence, HENRY, with marked indifference, walks to a
chair and sits down. There is a sharp knock on the door.
CAESAR looks at WHARTON, waiting for instructions.*)

WHARTON (*sighs*): Yes, Caesar, open the door. There is
naught else we can do . . . but pray.

SALLY: Wait, Caesar! (CAESAR *halts.*) Come, Franny, we
must try to keep them from this room! Peyton is bound
to recognize Henry, disguise or no disguise.

(*They exit with CAESAR, closing the door after them.
After a moment FRANNY and SALLY greet PEYTON in the
foyer offstage. WHARTON has walked up to the door to
listen.*)

FRANNY: Oh, Peyton! What a joy!

SALLY: Come in, Peyton! Come in!

PEYTON (*his voice hearty*): Franny! And Sally! How good
it is to see you both! (*There is the tramp of boots in the
foyer.*) You know Captain Lawton, I believe?

FRANNY: Yes, indeed! Welcome to The Locusts, sir.

LAWTON: Your servant, Miss Sally . . . Miss Frances.

SALLY: But do come into the dining room. I'll have Caesar
hurry up some refreshments for you.

PEYTON (*hesitantly*): Sally . . . this is not entirely a social
call, and we are pressed . . .

SALLY: Oh, tush, Peyton! Nothing is *that* pressing. Come,
now.

PEYTON: You are most kind. But, if you will excuse Captain
Lawton, he has instructions to give to the sergeant.

(*Their footsteps fade and go. WHARTON expels his
breath in relief. HENRY is still lounging in his chair with
utter indifference. There is a knock on the door. WHAR-
TON starts, holds his finger to his lips as he looks at
HENRY. The knock is repeated, then the door is opened
and CAPTAIN LAWTON enters, followed closely by the*

SERGEANT.)

LAWTON (*with deference*): Sorry to intrude, Mr. Wharton. I'm Captain Lawton.

WHARTON: Aye, what do you wish, sir?

LAWTON: I do regret this rude intrusion upon your privacy, sir, but the conditions of war make it necessary for me to ask you a few questions.

WHARTON (*coldly*): Pray, what questions, sir?

LAWTON: We have been informed that Harvey Birch . . . You know Harvey Birch, I'm sure?

WHARTON: I should. He is our neighbor.

LAWTON: Aye, sir, he is your neighbor. Have you seen him?

WHARTON: No, I have not seen him for many a day.

LAWTON (*as his eyes remain fastened on* HENRY *intently*): We were informed that he was seen in this locality. He is not in this house, sir?

WHARTON: Harvey Birch? Why, certainly not!

LAWTON (*his eyes still on* HENRY): Might I ask, then, whose horse is that standing ready saddled in the shed?

WHARTON (*floundering*): Why . . . why . . . this gentleman's . . . who favored us with his company during the rain storm of last evening.

LAWTON (*stepping forward toward* HENRY): Hmmm. (*With some lurking amusement*) This gentleman's, you say? I see. (*With a sense of comic gravity*) Your horse, sir?

HENRY (*looking up at him calmly*): Aye, my horse, sir.

LAWTON (*continuing in the same tone*): I perceive, sir, that you suffer from a severe cold in the head. My deepest sympathy, sir.

HENRY (*with a supercilious lift of his eyebrow*): I? I have no cold in my head.

LAWTON: No? Perhaps I fancied it then, from seeing your handsome black locks covered with that ugly wig. (WHARTON *is showing extreme anxiety, his face tense.*) But it was a mistake. You will please to pardon it, sir.

HENRY (*coldly*): It matters not, I assure you.

LAWTON (*extending his hand*): If you please, sir, may I examine the quality of your wig?

145

(HENRY *rises slowly to his feet, straightens up and looks*
LAWTON *boldly in the eye.*)

HENRY (*removing his wig and extending it to* LAWTON):
Certainly. Here you are. (*As* LAWTON *takes it*) I trust it is
to your liking?

LAWTON: Quite. Quite. But, if I may be permitted to say
so, sir, I prefer your ebony black hair. (*As* HENRY *looks at
him in cold silence*) Indeed, sir, that must have been a sad
hurt you received under that enormous black patch you
wear over your eye.

HENRY (*seething, but in perfect control*): You appear so
close an observer of things, I would welcome your opinion
of it, sir. (*He takes off his patch and hands it to* LAWTON
with a stiff bow.) Permit me.

LAWTON: Upon my word, but you do improve most rapidly
in externals. Now, if I could but persuade you to remove
that old cloak you are wearing . . .

HENRY: If that is your desire. (*He removes his cloak and
drops it on the floor.*)

LAWTON: What an amazing transformation, sir! (*Turning to*
SERGEANT) Is it not, sergeant?

SERGEANT: Indeed, yes, Captain.

LAWTON (*his tone changes to hardness*): And now, sir, since
it is usual for strangers to be introduced (*Bows stiffly*)
I am Captain Lawton of the Virginia horse.

HENRY (*bowing proudly*): And I, sir, am Captain Wharton
of his majesty's 60th regiment of foot.

(LAWTON *is taken completely by surprise. The* SERGEANT
emits a short whistle of astonishment. MR. WHARTON
groans his anguish.)

LAWTON (*after a long pause*): Henry Wharton. And I
thought . . .

SERGEANT (*breathes*): Holy Mary, Mither o' God!

WHARTON (*appealing*): Captain Lawton, do listen to me!
My son . . .

HENRY (*stops him with a grimace of distaste*): Oh, father,
please!

WHARTON (*To* LAWTON): Come, Captain Lawton, no need

146

to look so disappointed. Surely, an officer of his majesty is some compensation for failing to take Harvey Birch.

LAWTON (*with genuine pity*): I assure you, Captain Wharton, disappointment is not what I feel. I pity you. Pity you from the bottom of my heart. For, I'm very much afraid, you are going to hang for a spy.

WHARTON: Oh, no, no! My son is not a spy! He is merely on a visit to his home!

LAWTON: Sergeant, will you fetch, Major Dunwoodie? (*As the* SERGEANT *hesitates, nods towards* HENRY) I'm sure Captain Wharton is too much the gentleman to resort to violence within the confines of his own home. Fetch Major Dunwoodie. (*After the* SERGEANT *exits*) Captain Wharton, were you ignorant of the fact that our troops have been in this sector for several days?

HENRY (*sullenly*): I did not know until I reached them. Then it was too late to turn back.

LAWTON: All this may be true, sir. And then again . . .

WHARTON (*in proud anger*): A Wharton does not lie, sir!

LAWTON (*with considerable gentleness*): I did not say your son is lying, Mr. Wharton. But, when treason reaches the grade of general officers—as witness the affair of Major André—then it makes us very suspicious, and behooves us to be particularly vigilant.

> (LAWTON *turns to the door as he hears footsteps in the foyer. As* PEYTON *walks into the room and sees* HENRY, *his expression changes quickly from surprise to shock as he sizes up the situation.* MR. WHARTON *has sunk into a chair, looking miserable.* SALLY *and* FRANNY *trail in after* PEYTON. *As they move toward* HENRY *impulsively, he motions them back with a frown. The* SERGEANT *has stationed himself in the open doorway.*)

PEYTON (*shocked*): Henry! Henry, what in heavens name are you doing here?

HENRY (*laconically*): Paying a visit to my family.

PEYTON (*motions to his dress*): But you are not in uniform . . . (*Hoping against hope*) You've resigned from the king's service!

HENRY (scowling darkly): Never! Not while there is a single rebel bearing arms against my sovereign.

Peyton (frustrated): You utter fool! You bloody imbecile! Don't you realize what . . . (Stops, controls his anger, turns to LAWTON) Captain Lawton, will you be so good as to leave me alone with . . . (Hesitates to say it, but feels he must) with the prisoner.

(HENRY smiles sardonically, finding some gratification in PEYTON's discomfort. SALLY and FRANNY react to the word.)

SALLY (bitterly): Prisoner!

LAWTON: I understand, Major Dunwoodie. (He beckons to the SERGEANT, who follows him out of the room and closes the door.)

PEYTON: Henry, I . . . I am sorry we meet under such circumstances.

HENRY (hostile): Really? Most fortunate for you, is it not? It isn't every day you ran credit yourself with the capture of a British officer.

PEYTON (deeply hurt): Henry, for the love of heaven, don't take that tone with me!

FRANNY: Henry, please! I'm sure Peyton will do everything he can to help you . . . if . . .

HENRY: I don't recall asking for Major Dunwoodie's help, sister. (Turning to PEYTON) And it would please me very much if you addressed me henceforth as Captain Wharton. I must remind you, sir, you are addressing an officer of his Majesty, King George.

PEYTON (is about to retort sharply, but checks himself; coldly): Very well, Captain Wharton. Then, since you are my prisoner, I am obliged to ask you some questions.

HENRY (haughtily): I will be pleased to answer any questions . . . before a military tribunal.

PEYTON (loses patience): You witless fool! You . . .

SALLY (drawing herself up): Sir, you have no right to address my brother in that manner!

PEYTON (looking at her incredulously): What! (He is struck with the ludicrousness of her attitude, and begins to laugh mirthlessly as he presses his forehead with the palm of his hand.) Good Lord in heaven!

FRANNY (resentfully): Peyton Dunwoodie, I fail to see how you can find any humor in this situation!

PEYTON (looking at her sadly): No, I quite agree with you, there is nothing humorous in this situation. (He addresses all of them angrily.) Will you get it through your stubborn, proud heads that he will be doomed—doomed if he is brought to trial!

HENRY: I do not expect otherwise from hands stained with the blood of Major André.

(PEYTON looks at him for a moment with disgust, then, with a resigned, hopeless gesture, he goes to the door and opens it.)

PEYTON (calls out): Captain Lawton!

(He turns to look at FRANNY with appeal in his eyes. FRANNY turns her eyes away. LAWTON enters.)

LAWTON: Aye, Major?

PEYTON: Select a detachment and escort the prisoner to our headquarters in White Plains. Turn him over to Colonel Singleton and explain the circumstances of his capture. I will remain behind to continue the search for Harvey Birch.

LAWTON: Very good, sir. (To HENRY) Mr. Wharton . . . (Steps away from doorway) if you please. (HENRY stares at him coldly without budging.) Mr. Wharton!

HENRY (arrogantly): Are you by any chance addressing me, sir?

LAWTON (levelly): Yes, I am addressing you, sir.

HENRY: Then be so good to address me in the manner due an officer in his majesty's army.

LAWTON (looking him up and down): I see no evidence, sir, that you are an officer . . . or for that matter . . .

PEYTON (interrupts, scowling): Captain Lawton . . .

LAWTON: Yes, Major?

PEYTON (with a weary sigh): Oh, never mind. (Turning to HENRY) Please don't make it any more difficult than it is!

(HENRY looks at PEYTON coldly for a moment. With a shrug of his shoulders, he marches to the door and exits, closely followed by LAWTON. SALLY and MR. WHARTON turn to look at PEYTON with cold hostility. FRANNY seems to be weeping silently.)

WHARTON: Major Dunwoodie, I'm sure there is no further need for your presence in this house. It would please me greatly if you departed immediately! (PEYTON looks at him sadly, hurt.) Come, Sally . . . Frances. (He turns and walks to the door with SALLY following. FRANNY takes a couple of steps, then stops and turns to PEYTON. WHARTON is standing at the door. He steps aside to permit SALLY to leave. He speaks sharply to FRANNY.) Frances!

FRANNY: Please, father, I would like to have a word with Peyton.

WHARTON: Very well. But it is my wish that you make it very clear to Major Dunwoodie that he is no longer welcome under this roof, now and henceforth. Furthermore, his intended alliance with you no longer has my approval. (When WHARTON leaves, PEYTON strides back and forth in outrage and indignation. FRANNY watches him in deep distress.)

PEYTON: How unfair! How utterly unfair! (Walks a few steps) As if I . . . I were to blame for the abysmal, inexcusable stupidity of his son! (Stops before FRANNY; fiercely) And you, Franny . . . do you condone his attitude? Do you, too, hold me to blame for this unfortunate affair? (As FRANNY remains silent, PEYTON takes her hands and pleads.) Please, Franny . . .

FRANNY: No, I do not condone my father's attitude, nor do I hold you to blame. There is naught else you could have done under the circumstances.

PEYTON (kissing her hand in gratitude): Bless you, Franny. I knew I could count on you.

FRANNY: But, Peyton, I can understand my father's feelings, when you consider that his son's life hangs by a thread.

PEYTON: Nothing will happen to Henry. I will intercede for him!

FRANNY (*hopelessly*): Intercede? With whom, Peyton? With whom?

PEYTON: I am not without favor in the eyes of General Washington!

FRANNY: If entreaties could move him, would Major André have died on the gallows?

PEYTON: Major André was captured with documents concealed on his person, exposing the plot of that traitor, Benedict Arnold, to surrender West Point into British hands. Henry was not on a spying mission. Just one of those rash ventures he was ever so prone to indulge in, with no regard for the consequences! That's Henry, blast him! (*Pacing back and forth*) When he appears for trial before a military tribunal, if it could be proven that he saw no one, *spoke* with no one, and showed no indication of spying from the time he left the British lines to his arrival here, then . . .

FRANNY: There is only one who could testify to that, Peyton! (*With bitter certainty*) But I can't see him placing *his* neck in the halter to save Henry's life.

PEYTON: Who are you talking about, Franny?

FRANNY (*doesn't know what a bombshell she is dropping*): Harvey Birch.

PEYTON (*startled*): Who?!

FRANNY: It was Harvey Birch who led Henry through the American lines.

PEYTON (*shocked, groans*): Oh, no! (*Sinks into chair*) Oh, no!

FRANNY (*puzzled by his reaction*): But, Peyton, what difference does that make?

PEYTON (*rising*): What difference does that make, you ask? Good God, Franny. Don't you realize what effect it will have on a military tribunal when they hear that Harvey Birch, a known spy in the pay of the British, led him through the American lines?

FRANNY (*miserable*): Yes, I see. How right you are. (*Demands*) But why need they?

PEYTON (*hoping not to hear the answer he expects*): Why

need they *what*, Franny?

FRANNY: Why need they know?

PEYTON (*stares at her for a moment*): If only you hadn't told me!

FRANNY: Why not? Surely, you don't feel obliged to stand against him when he comes to trial?

PEYTON: No, but I expect to stand *for* him! And, as an officer in the American army, I am in duty bound to tell all the facts as I know them! I am in honor bound . . .

FRANNY (*interrupts vehemently*): Your duty! Your honor! Does it mean more to you than the life of my brother?

PEYTON (*trying to draw her close to him*): Oh, Franny, Franny, don't you see the position I am in?

FRANNY (*breaking away angrily*): Don't you dare touch me, Peyton Dunwoodie!

PEYTON (*pleads*): Franny . . .

FRANNY: And if you expect me to marry a man whose hands may very well help hang my own brother . . . (*Stops, almost in tears.*)

   PEYTON *regards her for a moment, deeply hurt. He turns away, starts walking towards the door.* FRANNY *watches him go; but when he reaches the door, she calls out and runs towards him.*)

FRANNY: Peyton! Peyton, wait! (*She runs into his arms, weeping.*) Forgive me, Peyton. I . . . I would be the first to despise you . . . if . . . if you put honor and duty aside.

PEYTON (*tenderly*): We must not give up hope, my dear Franny. I will do everything humanly possible to intercede for him. I will talk with General Washington himself and try to explain . . . (FRANNY *is not listening. She has just remembered something, interrupts.*)

FRANNY: Peyton, do you know anyone by the name of John Harper?

PEYTON (*astonished*): Who? Who did you say?

FRANNY: John Harper. He . . .

PEYTON: How do you know John Harper?

FRANNY: Why, he came to us as a stranger last night, seeking shelter from the storm. It was *he* who warned Henry . . .

PEYTON: What! He met Henry?

FRANNY: Indeed, yes. Mr. Harper penetrated his disguise . . .

PEYTON: You mean he knew him as a British officer?

FRANNY: Yes, and promised to help Henry if he were taken.

PEYTON (*highly excited*): He did?

FRANNY: But, Peyton, do you know him? Who is he? Has he any power to help my brother?

PEYTON (*joyfully*): Can he! If he cannot, who can? (*Remembers, groans*) Oh, but where to find him! Where to find him in time . . . before . . . (*Kisses her quickly*) Goodbye, Franny! This cannot be delayed! I must find your Mr. Harper! (*He turns and quickly departs.*)

    (FRANNY *walks to a chair. In despair, she bows her head in her hands. After a pause,* HARVEY BIRCH, *disguised as a clergyman, appears in the doorway. He seems to have just come down the stairs from the upper floor to the foyer. His back is turned to* FRANNY *as he cautiously peers into the other room.* FRANNY, *her head still bowed, is unaware of his presence.* HARVEY *turns to face her, his face wearing a lopsided grin as he chews on a long straw. He looks at* FRANNY *sympathetically. Suddenly, with a grimace, he begins to scratch himself vigorously. He stops his scratching to address* FRANNY.)

HARVEY: Now, now, Miss Frances . . . don't take on so.

    (FRANNY's *head comes up with a startled jerk. She springs to her feet in alarm.*)

FRANNY: Harvey Birch! Where . . . ? (HARVEY *thrusts his hand down the back of his neck and begins to scratch again.*)

HARVEY: Drat that hay! Nothing will bring on a worser itch than lyin' in a hayloft!

FRANNY (*demands*): What are you doing in this house? How did you get in here?

HARVEY: Been in the hayloft over the carriage shed, Miss Frances. As you know, there's a door leadin' from there into the attic.

FRANNY: You wretched spy! If . . . if it were not for you . . .

    (*With determination in her stride, she begins to walk*

153

quickly to the door. HARVEY *stops her.*)

HARVEY (*restraining her gently*): Now, Miss Frances, wait, will ye? Just hear me through afore you start hollering for the sojers, if that's what you have a mind to do.

FRANNY: I most certainly do!

HARVEY (*looking over his shoulder*): Hush, Miss Frances! If you want me to help get that brother of yours out of the fix he's in, you'll listen to me.

FRANNY (*contemptuously*): You? How can you help him!

HARVEY: Couldn't help hear what you and the major were saying. Was just at the top of the stairs . . .

FRANNY (*outraged*): How contemptible! To eavesdrop . . .

HARVEY (*cheerfully*): Ain't it now? (*Sighs*) But I always was a nosey kind of critter. Seems like I always want to know things. Like where Mr. Harper might be . . . for instance?

FRANNY (*regarding him narrowly*): I don't believe you, Harvey Birch!

HARVEY (*sighs*): Ah, well . . . holler for the sojers. Can't say I didn't try. (*As* FRANNY *seems to waver*) But, I'm the only one on God's earth who knows where he is at this moment. So, if you want to put your trust in a no-account scoundrel like Harvey Birch, I'll lead you to him, Miss Frances.

SCENE 3

It is two days later. A large room in a manor house has been requisitioned as headquarters for the American army under the command of General George Washington. Left front, a long table with three chairs facing right. A big Bible rests on the table. Another chair, at the end of the table toward the back, faces front. An inkpot and quills are on the table for the use of the court clerk. A thirteen-starred American flag hangs on the wall behind the chairs. Several chairs front center for spectators. There are two entrances to the room right center and left back.

At curtain rise SALLY *and* MR. WHARTON *are seated together, talking and casting anxious glances towards entrance right.* PEYTON *and* LAWTON *are standing down center engaged in low conversation. Stationed near each entrance is an American* SOLDIER, *standing at rest.*

LAWTON: Where is Miss Frances, Major? (*Wondering*) Is she not expected to stand for her brother?
PEYTON (*unhappily*): I don't know, Captain Lawton. (*As* LAWTON *looks towards the* WHARTONS *with a puzzled frown,* PEYTON, *noting it, smiles wryly.*)
LAWTON (*quizzically*): Oh?
PEYTON: Yes, I am out of favor— completely out of favor— with the house of Wharton.
LAWTON: Sorry to hear that. (*Scowls*) And, if you'll forgive the presumption, sir, decidedly unfair, I must say.
PEYTON (*nodding regretfully*): And yet, one can understand their feelings.
LAWTON (*hesitantly*): And . . . Miss Frances, sir?
PEYTON: I trust she does not share their feelings. But she *is* Mr. Wharton's daughter, and (*Sighs, tries to cast it off with a shrug*) Oh, well . . . (*With bitter disappointment*) If only I could have found him! It's almost as if he had completely vanished from the face of the earth!
LAWTON: Who, sir?
PEYTON: The one man who has, without a question of doubt, the power to save Henry Wharton's fool neck!
(*The* CLERK *of the court, a sergeant in uniform, enters from door left back. Rolled up under his arm are the articles of* HENRY's *disguise. He carries a folder in his hand. As he enters, the* SOLDIERS *stiffen to attention. All eyes turn to the door.* SALLY *and* MR. WHARTON *rise. The* CLERK *deposits the clothing, etc. on the end of the table as the three American* OFFICERS *who are to judge* HENRY *enter the room from door left back. First to enter is the acting chief judge,* COLONEL SINGLETON. *Behind him, as they enter, a* MAJOR *and a* CAPTAIN. *They all are wearing uniforms of the Continental Army. As they seat themselves, with the Colonel in the middle, the* CLERK *walks in front of the table, places the folio*

before the COLONEL, and opens it. He returns to his place at the end of the table, seats himself, examines his quills, starts trimming one or two of the quills with a small knife.)

COLONEL: Be seated, please. (*To* SOLDIERS) At ease, soldiers. (*He studies the papers before him, has a short consultation with his associates.* SALLY *and* MR. WHARTON *are casting anxious glances toward the entrance right. The* COLONEL *looks up at the* WHARTONS *with sympathy.*) I believe, sir, you are Mr. Wharton, father to the prisoner, Henry Wharton?

WHARTON: Aye, sir.

COLONEL: And you, young lady?

SALLY (*answering with pride and defiance in her voice, placing a slight emphasis on "Captain."*): I, Sir, am Sarah Wharton, sister to Captain Henry Wharton, a loyal officer in his majesty's service.

(*The three judges react in different ways to* SALLY's *provocative answer. The* COLONEL, *the oldest of the three, smiles with sympathetic amusement. The* CAPTAIN, *who is quite young, as a matter of duty, feels impelled to frown sternly at* SALLY, *then looks at the* COLONEL, *expecting him to reprimand her. The* MAJOR *has a quizzical lift to his brow as he looks at the* COLONEL. MR. WHARTON *stirs uneasily, whispers sharply to* SALLY. *She responds with a defiant toss of her head.*)

COLONEL (*looking down at the paper*): Ah, yes, Miss Sarah Wharton. (*Looks up*) Mr. Wharton, it is our understanding that another daughter of yours (*Looks down at paper*) Miss Frances Wharton, was summoned to appear as a witness before this court.

WHARTON: True, sir. I beg your indulgence for her absence.

COLONEL: She is not well, perhaps?

WHARTON: No, sir, that is not the case. She . . . she left shortly after my . . . my son was taken, to seek a Mr. Harper. (*The name, evidently, means nothing to the judges. But,* PEYTON, *startled, half rises from his seat to stare at* WHARTON.)

PEYTON: What! (WHARTON *throws a quick glance at him, then turns his eyes away coldly.* PEYTON, *with a puzzled look, sinks back in his seat.*)

COLONEL: What concern has this Mr. Harper in this matter, if any?

WHARTON: Mr. John Harper was present when my son Henry arrived at our home in White Plains. He knows, and can attest, that my son's only purpose in undertaking that unfortunate journey was to see his family. We had hoped Mr. Harper could be here to witness for my son . . . (*With a sad gesture*) But, alas, sir, my daughter, evidently, has failed to find him, and we know not where she may be. Indeed, we are deeply concerned for her safety.

COLONEL: We are sorry to hear that, Mr. Wharton, for we would wish to see the prisoner given the utmost assistance in his behalf. (*Turning to* SOLDIER *at entrance left.*) We will proceed. Have the prisoner brought forth. (*The* SOLDIER *salutes, wheels and exits.*)

PEYTON (*stands*): If you please, Colonel Singleton.

COLONEL: Yes, Major Dunwoodie?

PEYTON: May I petition the court to disqualify me as a witness in this matter, sir?

COLONEL (*highly displeased*): I pray you, on what grounds, sir?

PEYTON: I am, and have been for many years standing, a close friend of the Wharton family. In fact, sir, I am at present affianced . . . (*He throws a glance at the* WHARTONS, *who pointedly ignore his presence.* PEYTON, *his jaw outthrust, repeats for their benefit.*) Yes, affianced to Miss Frances Wharton. Under those circumstances, sir, I can not help but be biased, and my testimony open to question.

CAPTAIN (*with cold disapproval*): Indeed, Major Dunwoodie, your duty to your country comes first. As an officer in the American Army, you must put aside all personal feelings in this matter to see justice done.

PEYTON (*pleads*): But I am firmly convinced of his innocence!

157

COLONEL (*sharply*): Major Dunwoodie, you are out of order! Outrageously so, I might add!

PEYTON (*looking down*): I beg the forgiveness of the court, sir.

COLONEL: It is highly improper for you to offer any opinion of either his guilt or innocence at this moment!

(*The* SOLDIER *appears at door left. He enters and steps to the left of the doorway to permit* HENRY *to enter. A* THIRD SOLDIER *brings up the rear. He enters and moves to flank* HENRY *on the right.* HENRY's *shoulders are back, his head held proudly. He smiles at* SALLY *and* MR. WHARTON. *The two* SOLDIERS *and* HENRY *stand and wait for orders.*)

COLONEL: Major Dunwoodie. Your plea is denied. Will the prisoner step forward and face the court?

(HENRY *steps up and faces the judges. The two* SOLDIERS *station themselves on each side of entrance, left.*)

(*NOTE: The scene would be greatly enhanced with a body of spectators present and reacting to the proceedings. But, if production limitations preclude this, cut the following speech of the* COLONEL's *and the entrance of the* SPECTATORS, *and pick up at the order to close the doors.*)

COLONEL (*to* SOLDIER *guarding entrance right*): If there are any outside who wish to witness the proceedings, they may enter now. (*The* SOLDIER *steps to the door and motions the* SPECTATORS *to come in. The* SPECTATORS *enter. Most of them are American officers; some bearing evidence of wounds. When they are all seated, the* COLONEL *orders the* SOLDIERS *to close the doors.*) Close the doors and permit no further entrance.

(*As the* SOLDIER *at the right entrance is about to shut the door, we hear* FRANNY's *voice offstage.*)

FRANNY (*breathless*): If you please, sir!

(SALLY, WHARTON *and* PEYTON *rise as* FRANNY *rushes in. They all look immensely relieved, hardly notice that*

HARVEY BIRCH, *still disguised as a clergyman, enters after her and unobtrusively seats himself in the rear. But* HENRY, *who is familiar with* HARVEY's *disguise, sees him, looks with wonderment and amusement at* HARVEY.)

WHARTON (*with great relief to judges*): My daughter Frances, gentlemen.

(As FRANNY *passes by* PEYTON, *he looks at her with a marked expression of inquiry.* FRANNY *smiles at him and nods her head vigorously, then seats herself to the right of her father. The* WHARTONS *engage in hurried whispers.* PEYTON's *face expresses bewilderment as he looks at* FRANNY.)

COLONEL: Let us proceed. (*To* HENRY) You are said to be Henry Wharton, a captain in his Britannic Majesty's 60th regiment of foot.

HENRY: I am.

MAJOR: Colonel Singleton.

COLONEL: Yes, Major?

MAJOR: It would be prudent, and in order, to advise the prisoner that he is bound to answer no more than he deems necessary; for, although we are a court of martial law, yet, in this respect, we follow the principles of all free governments.

COLONEL: Thank you, Major Pendleton. Will you please bear that in mind, Captain Wharton?

HENRY: Thank you, sir, I shall. But, I assure you I have nothing to hide.

COLONEL (*drily*): Your candor does you credit, sir. (*He refers to the paper.*) The accusation against you is as follows: You, an officer of the enemy, on the 29th of October last, passed the pickets of the American Army while wearing a disguise. Whereby, you are suspected of actions hostile to the interests of the American cause, and, thereby, under the rules of war, subjected yourself to punishment accorded a spy. (*Pauses*) What have you to say to the charge, Captain Wharton?

HENRY: That I passed your pickets in disguise . . . that, I do

not deny. But, that I had any intent to spy when I did so
. . . that is *not* true, sir.

COLONEL: What was your intention then, pray?

HENRY: To see my family.

COLONEL: Prior to this visit, how long a period had elapsed
since you saw them last?

HENRY: More than a year, I would say.

COLONEL: I see. And on your previous visit, did you at that
time travel in disguise?

HENRY: No, sir. I was in uniform.

COLONEL: Why, may I inquire?

HENRY (*cautiously*): Well . . . because that sector was occupied by his majesty's forces at that time.

COLONEL: I see. (*Narrowly*) But this time you felt the need
to practice deceit.

HENRY: Deceit, sir?

COLONEL: Aye, what else would you call it when you disguise
your true identity as a British officer, sir?

HENRY: I would call it *prudence*, sir, to guard against capture
by my enemies.

MAJOR (*sharply*): A soldier, Captain Wharton, should ever
meet his enemy openly, and with arms in his hands. I have
served two kings of England, sir, as I now serve my native
land. But never, sir, never have I approached a foe without
giving honest notice that I came as his enemy.

(HENRY *decides not to answer, turns sullen.*)

COLONEL (*nodding to* HENRY's *disguise on table*): Captain
Wharton, may I call your attention to the articles there
on the table. (HENRY *nods, looks at articles.*) Will you
please place them upon your person.

HENRY (*his face tight with resentment*): Is that at all necessary, gentlemen?

COLONEL: We deem it so. (HENRY *dresses himself in the
disguise, scowling, as the judges put their heads together in
consultation.*) Now, Captain Wharton, will you turn and
face the people. (HENRY *turns, tight-lipped with anger and
humiliation.*) Captain Lawton!

LAWTON (*stands*): Aye, Colonel?

COLONEL: Was Captain Wharton dressed as you see him when he was apprehended on October 29 last?

LAWTON: He was, sir.

COLONEL: Were you aware of his true identity before he removed his disguise?

LAWTON: No, sir. In truth, Colonel, I thought I had taken that cursed spy, Harvey Birch, until Captain Wharton acknowledged his true identity.

COLONEL (*surprised*): You say he *acknowledged* his true identity?

LAWTON: Yes, and quite freely I must say, Colonel.

COLONEL (*looking at* HENRY, *seems favorably impressed*): Indeed. Did you interrogate the prisoner at that time?

LAWTON: No, sir. I summoned Major Dunwoodie.

COLONEL: Thank you, Captain Lawton. (LAWTON *bows and sits down.*) Major Dunwoodie, will you come forward please? (PEYTON *rises, steps forward. The* COLONEL *turns to* HENRY.) You may remove those articles, Captain Wharton. (*He notes the repugnance with which* HENRY *drops each article on the table, one by one.*) Yes, I agree with you, sir. They are most unbecoming to you. (*Turning to* PEYTON.) Major Dunwoodie, you interrogated the prisoner on the occasion of his capture?

PEYTON: I tried to, sir, but quite unsuccessfully. He insisted he would only answer questions put to him before a military tribunal.

COLONEL (*looking at* HENRY *grimly*): I see. Then the prisoner did, evidently, expect to be tried for a spy.

PEYTON: Colonel Singleton, may I be permitted to make a statement at this moment?

COLONEL: You may.

PEYTON: I truly believe, sir, that Captain Wharton's sole motive was to visit his family. He has always had the deepest affection for them, and must have missed them sorely.

CAPTAIN (*skeptically*): Even at the risk of being captured and hanged as a spy?

PEYTON: Knowing him as I do . . . and that, since childhood

. . . I would say, yes. Rash . . . impulsive . . . yes. But, a liar . . . never, captain. And, if he says that he was not on a spying mission, I, for one, believe him.

CAPTAIN (*with a detectable sneer*): Major Dunwoodie seems to hold the prisoner in considerable esteem, I must say. Most remarkable, considering that he is a Tory officer.

(*The* COLONEL's *face shows displeasure at the uncalled for remark of his colleague.*)

COLONEL (*dismissing* PEYTON *quickly*): Thank you, Major Dunwoodie. (PEYTON *goes back to his seat as the* COLONEL *turns to* HENRY.) Captain Wharton, on investigation we learned that as you crossed the White Plains road you were halted by an American picket. Is that true?

HENRY: That is true.

COLONEL: You showed him a pass. And on the strength of that pass he permitted you to continue. Is that true?

HENRY: That is true.

COLONEL: And it was the same pass that we found on your person when you were searched, Captain Wharton?

HENRY: It was, sir.

COLONEL (*picks up the pass from the table and hands it to* HENRY): Is this the same pass, Captain Wharton?

HENRY (*after examining the pass*): Yes, I believe it is, sir.

COLONEL: And whose signature is affixed to the bottom of the pass?

HENRY (*amused*): General George Washington.

COLONEL (*severely*): How did you come by that pass, sir?

HENRY (*dismissing it with a shrug*): Does it matter, really? The signature is obviously a forgery. (*He hands the pass back to the* COLONEL.)

COLONEL (*levelly*): On the contrary, sir, the signature is not a forgery . . . it is in the true hand of General Washington.

HENRY (*with a laugh of disbelief*): It couldn't be! It couldn't possibly be!

COLONEL (*firmly*): But, I assure you it is. (*Summons* PEYTON) Major Dunwoodie, will you come forward please. (PEYTON *steps up to the table. The* COLONEL *hands him the pass.*) Major, you have been aide to General Washington for quite some time now, have you not?

PEYTON: I would say for a goodly part of two years, sir.

COLONEL: Then you must be quite familiar with his signature.

PEYTON: True, sir. I have prepared many letters and documents for him to sign.

COLONEL: Would you say that is his true signature on that pass?

(PEYTON *examines the pass carefully. He looks up with dismay and puzzlement at* HENRY.)

COLONEL (*impatiently*): Well, Major Dunwoodie?

PEYTON (*reluctantly*): Yes, Colonel Singleton, it is in the general's hand. In fact, sir, I myself wrote out this pass at the request of General Washington, and saw him sign it. (*This causes quite a stir in the courtroom.* PEYTON *hands the pass back to the* COLONEL.)

COLONEL: Thank you, Major Dunwoodie.

(PEYTON *returns to his seat.* HENRY *has been stealing covert glances at* HARVEY. HARVEY'S *eyes are fastened on the ceiling, his face wearing a lopsided grin.* HENRY *rubs his face thoughtfully, smiling as he regards* HARVEY. *It appears as if something about* HARVEY, *which had puzzled him before, is beginning to clear up.* HENRY *is so absorbed in thought, he doesn't respond immediately to the* COLONEL'S *next question.*)

COLONEL: Do you still have any doubts that the signature is genuine, Captain Wharton? . . . (*Sharply*) Captain Wharton!

HENRY (*starts*): Your pardon, sir. No, I don't in the least doubt now that the signature is genuine.

COLONEL. And what more have you to say to that, sir?

HENRY (*murmurs*): I find it very interesting . . . very interesting, indeed.

COLONEL (*exasperated*): Is that all you have to say, just very interesting? (HENRY *doesn't answer, just shrugs his shoulders.*) Where did you get this pass, sir?

HENRY (*insouciantly*): It was loaned to me.

COLONEL (*demands*): By whom, I pray you?

HENRY (*indifferently*): By Harvey Birch.
(*The judges are shocked, then their faces turn grim. The* WHARTONS *are extremely disturbed.* MR. WHARTON *leans forward, his eyes closed, shaking his head hopelessly.*)
COLONEL (*grimly*): Harvey Birch, aye?
MAJOR: By the saints . . . !
CAPTAIN: Harvey Birch! Indeed, sir!
MAJOR (*flabbergasted*): You freely admit that Harvey Birch loaned you this pass?
HENRY (*restraining a smile*): Quite freely, sir. In fact, I am pleased to add, he even accompanied me through the American lines.
COLONEL: Were you aware at that time that Harvey Birch was, and is, a wretched spy?
HENRY: But of course. (*The* COLONEL *sits back in amazement at* HENRY's *candor, then he shakes his head pityingly.*)
COLONEL (*gravely*): I'm afraid, Captain Wharton, very much afraid, you have just . . .
HENRY (*as if continuing*): But . . . what I didn't know . . . at that time . . . was, that he is a spy in the pay of the Americans, not the British. (*Scowling*). And if he ever does hang for a spy . . . by God's blood! . . it will be with British hemp around his neck, not American!
COLONEL: Are you implying, sir, that Harvey Birch is a spy in the service of the American cause?
HENRY: Aye, and I'm quite sure of it now.
CAPTAIN (*scoffing*): Surely, you don't hope to have us believe such a ridiculous allegation?
HENRY: Not at all, captain. But, if Harvey Birch could be questioned . . . ?
CAPTAIN (*sarcastically*): But of course. All we have to do is issue a call for Harvey Birch and he'll hasten to oblige you. Just happy to put his head in a noose!
HENRY: Oh, I don't think you should have any difficulty on that score, sir.
COLONEL (*aroused*): Sir, it ill behooves you to trifle with us!

Or perhaps you don't realize that your very life is at stake?

HENRY: I assure you, gentlemen, I am not trifling. And if you will permit me the liberty . . . (*He looks at* HARVEY, *beckons him with a crooked finger.*) Harvey, my good friend and kind neighbor, would you be so good as to oblige the gentlemen? (HARVEY *stands and ambles up toward the* Judges. HENRY *bows mockingly to* HARVEY.) The Right Reverend Harvey Birch, gentlemen.

COLONEL (*glaring at* HENRY): And this . . . this clergyman you claim is Harvey Birch?

HENRY: I beg you not to be misled by his Godly garments.

COLONEL: Your name, sir!

HARVEY: Harvey Birch, Colonel.

The SOLDIERS *make an involuntary move toward him. The* COLONEL *waves them back.*)

COLONEL: What say you to the statement that the prisoner just made . . . that you have been operating as a spy in the service of the American command?

HARVEY (*scratching his chin thoughtfully as he reflects on the point*): Well now, sir . . . can't say I have . . . nor can't say I haven't.

COLONEL (*out of patience*): What manner of answer is that! Either you have, or you haven't!

HARVEY: Don't mean to get your bile a-boilin', Colonel. But . . . you see it be this way. Can't tell you one way or t'other, 'thout permission.

COLONEL: Permission from whom, in heaven's name?

HARVEY: From the gentleman that ordered me to appear here and lend a hand, come necessary.

COLONEL (*scowling*): Would it be too much to ask who that gentleman is?

HARVEY (*extremely obliging*): Not a-tall, Colonel, not a-tall! Name is Mr. John Harper, sir.

COLONEL (*completely out of patience*): In the name of God and all his angels! Who *is* this Mr. Harper?

FRANNY (*rising and speaking up, timidly*). He is the gentleman, sir, who spent the night with us when . . .

COLONEL (*controlling his irritation*): Yes, yes, Miss Wharton, so I have been informed. But . . .

FRANNY (*with a rush of words*): And he's outside waiting to be called if you deem it necessary. (*She sits down with haste.*)

COLONEL: Indeed? Outside, where?

FRANNY (*popping up again*): Outside this room, sir. (*She sits down again with the same haste.*)

COLONEL (*with a weary sigh, calls to the* SOLDIER *standing at door right*): Will you see if there is a Mr. John Harper outside? (*The* SOLDIER *salutes, half opens the door and calls out.*)

SOLDIER: John Harper! Is there one John Harper among ye? If there be such . . .

(*The* SOLDIER *stops suddenly, opens the door wide, stiffens to attention with a salute.* GENERAL GEORGE WASHINGTON *walks in. He is in full uniform. Everyone stands as he walks to the table, saluting his officers with a smile as he goes by, amid a surprised and excited murmur of voices: "It's the General! . . . General Washington!"* FRANNY, *her eyes open wide with incredulity and surprise, leans on the back of the chair for support, her other hand covering her mouth, as her eyes follow his progress to the table. When* WASHINGTON *reaches the table, the* SPECTATORS *get seated again, but the judges are still standing.* WASHINGTON *bows deeply, in respect for their function as a military tribunal.*)

WASHINGTON (*with insistence, apologetic*): Gentlemen, do be seated. I'm truly sorry to disrupt your proceedings, but (*With a slight smile*) I was summoned to appear before the court by the guard.

COLONEL (*with a puzzled look as he rubs his forehead*): Forgive us, General Washington, if we appear somewhat confused . . .

WASHINGTON (*with a broad smile*): It is quite understandable, Colonel. But, if anyone needs to be forgiven, it is myself. (*Turning to* WHARTONS) Especially so, by Mr. Wharton and his charming daughters, upon whom I practiced such deceit; which, indeed, was ill return for

166

their gracious hospitality. (*Turning back to judges*) Your servant, gentlemen.

COLONEL: It has been stated, General, that you had occasion to meet the prisoner before.

WASHINGTON: That is true, sir . . . on the evening prior to his capture.

COLONEL: Was it your impression that his sole motive in making his way through the American lines was to visit his family?

WASHINGTON: I am quite certain he did so in all innocence of spying, Colonel. (*Turning to look at* HARVEY.) But, there is none better qualified to verify that than our friend here, Harvey Birch, who accompanied him on the journey.

COLONEL (*eyeing* HARVEY *severely as he picks up the pass*): And, I believe, without authority, gave him this pass.

WASHINGTON (*with tempered severity*): And that, gentlemen, is a matter that I still have to take up with Harvey Birch. (*He frowns at* HARVEY, *but a ghost of a smile is on his lips.*) Hmm . . . yes indeed. Nevertheless, I welcome this chance to expose him publicly. (*He addresses all.*) When an American soldier goes into battle, ready to lay down his life in the cause of human liberty, we honor him . . . and justly so. But, how shall we regard a man who not only is ready to sacrifice his life in a just cause, but sacrifice his good name, his honor, and his respect in the eyes of his countrymen and neighbors, receiving nothing in return but contempt and hatred for the service he renders his country? (*Pauses to look at* HARVEY, *who is grinning and quite abashed.*) Such a man is Harvey Birch, my friends. And he would have continued to serve me so, if (*He indicates court*) he hadn't created this situation, and so terminated his usefulness (*Smiles*) to John Harper. But, perhaps, God so willed it. For, I assure you, gentlemen, I would not have rested easy in the thought, that I, and I alone, could clear his name. And if, perchance, anything happened to me, he would, for the rest of his miserable life, be shunned like a leper by his countrymen, and go down in history as a traitor to his people.

THE SPY

COLONEL: Thank you, General Washington. In consideration of your assurance . . . (He stops) You may be seated, Mr. Birch. (HARVEY *wastes no time in moving away to find a seat.*) On your assurance, General, that Captain Wharton's venture through the American lines was but to see his family, this tribunal herewith frees him of the charge of spying in the service of the British command. We establish his status as a prisoner of war; and he is to be held as such in the prison stockade at West Point. (*He stands up to indicate the case is closed. The other two judges follow suit. The* SPECTATORS *begin to leave amid a buzz of conversation.*)

WASHINGTON: Colonel Singleton, it would please me very much if Captain Wharton were paroled . . . perhaps in the custody of Major Dunwoodie here . . . until a suitable exchange can be arranged with Sir Henry Clinton, his commander.

SINGLETON: So be it ordered, General Washington.

(*As the judges exit, the* WHARTONS, *overcome with gratitude, walk up to* WASHINGTON. HENRY *remains aside, biting his lip, in conflict with himself.* PEYTON *looks at him, starts to make a tentative move in his direction but stops.* HARVEY *is standing at quite a distance from the others, closely observing their attitudes.*)

WHARTON (*with a break in his voice*): It is impossible for me to find words to thank you, General Washington . . .

WASHINGTON: Not at all, Mr. Wharton. I would have been deeply grieved if your son had suffered the fate of a spy for his rashness. (*Looks at* FRANNY *somberly*) And were it not for this little lady warning me in time . . . (*He shakes his head gravely as he looks at* HENRY) he very well might have hanged at that.

HENRY (*with a bow*): My deepest respect and gratitude, General Washington, for the kindness and consideration you have shown me and my family. (*He looks at* PEYTON.) I ill deserve it. (*Looks at* WASHINGTON) And may I add, sir, that if, perchance, his majesty's forces do not prevail in this struggle, then at least the American colonies,

168

I trust, will remain in the hands of men of honor like yourself, sir.

WASHINGTON (*smiling*): Such tribute from a British officer does my heart good, Captain. Perhaps, some day, under happier circumstances, I may have the pleasure of enjoying the hospitality of your home again.

SALLY: You will afford us the greatest honor if you do so, General Washington.

WASHINGTON (*smiling broadly*): And I will look forward to being received as plain Mr. Washington, not as that rebel general, George Washington, masquerading as John Harper, Miss Wharton.

SALLY (*casting down her eyes in embarrassment*): No matter what you may choose to call yourself in the future, you will be regarded by *all* of us as a noble and generous man, sir.

WASHINGTON: You are most kind, Miss Wharton. Major Dunwoodie, you have my leave to escort Captain Wharton and his family to their home. (*Bows*) I bid you all a pleasant journey.

HENRY (*holding out his wrists to* PEYTON *with a laugh*): What, no gyves, chains or shackles, Peyton?

PEYTON (*smiling at him*): Sorry, Henry, I just happen to be without them at the moment. But, if you insist. . . ?

HENRY: Not at all! (*Seriously*) I would much rather have my hand free . . . to shake yours . . . if you feel so inclined, Peyton?

> (PEYTON *moves forward to shake* HENRY'S *hand. In the interval*, HARVEY *begins to sidle out toward the door.* WASHINGTON *sees him.*)

WASHINGTON (*calling out*): Harvey Birch! (HARVEY *stops in his tracks and turns around.*)

HARVEY: Aye, general? (*He looks like a boy expecting a scolding as he walks back.*)

WASHINGTON (*with pretended severity*): And where do you think you're off to?

HARVEY: Just thought I'd get to home and start gettin' my winter warmin' wood in. Goin' to be a mighty cold winter, I hear tell, general.

WASHINGTON: Sorry, I have other plans for you Harvey.

HARVEY (*relieved*): Then you ain't cross with me, general?

WASHINGTON: Cross as can be, Harvey.

HARVEY (*hanging his head*): 'Twas just a . . .

WASHINGTON: I know . . . just a neighborly act. So you told me. Nevertheless, I'm going to make sure that the British never get their hands on you. For if they ever do . . . (*Shakes his head dolefully.*)

HENRY (*finishing for him*): They'd hang him to the nearest tree. And that, I must say, as well deserved as it might be, I would not care to see.

WASHINGTON (*bowing low*): Ladies and gentlemen . . . I bid you all good day.

(SALLY *and* FRANNY *are in a deep curtsy, as the men bow.*)

CURTAIN

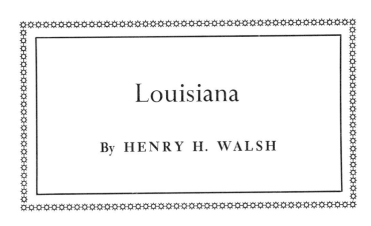

Louisiana

By HENRY H. WALSH

LOUISIANA

CHARACTERS: 11 males; 1 female

PLAYING TIME: 60 minutes

SETS: Three

✌️ Historical Notes

The three scenes in the play are imaginary, but the sub-
stantive material from which they are drawn is quite valid:
Napoleon's motive in selling the Louisiana Territory; the
question of international legality and the lack of United
States constitutional authority; the relevance to the Burr
conspiracy; the threat of secession of New York and New
England; the early forecast of the Civil War, and Jefferson's
personal dilemma and conflict.

It takes no more than a glance at the map of North
America for the year 1800 to see the untenable position in
which the young United States would have found itself if
France had taken formal possession of the Louisiana Terri-
tory at that time. To the north were the British in Canada.
To the south were the Spanish in Florida, the Gulf of
Mexico, and Mexico which extended north along the Pacific
coast to meet the British position in the Pacific Northwest.
Both Britain and Spain thus blocked the advance of the
United States to the Pacific coast. The all-powerful British
fleet ruled the Atlantic, and was a constant threat to our
east coast and our expanding commerce with Europe and the
West Indies.

The clash with one or the other (or all) would have been
inevitable. And it did result in war with England in 1812,
and with Mexico in 1846. What would have happened if
France had remained in possession of the Louisiana Territory
and New Orleans is a matter for fascinating speculation.
Certainly, it is highly unlikely that the English would have
permitted France to remain in possession of the territory
for long. Would we, then, have found ourselves allied with

England against our friend France? If so, would we have been involved in the Napoleonic Wars? Could we possibly have forced a powerful nation like England out of the Louisiana Territory? Or were we as a nation destined, come what may, to spread "from the rock-bound coast of Maine, to the sun-kissed shores of California" . . . All these are fascinating points for speculation, for never in the history of our nation were there so many "if's" as there were in the year 1803, when we acquired the Louisiana Territory and doubled the geographic size of the nation.

✌️ Production Notes

⟪ Characters

JEB DENBY, *First trapper*
BILL DAWSON, *Second trapper*
CHESTER COREY, *Third trapper*
MERIWETHER LEWIS, *Thomas Jefferson's private secretary*
THOMAS JEFFERSON, *President of the United States*
JAMES MONROE, *later to be the fifth President of the United States*
AARON BURR, *Vice-President of the United States under Thomas Jefferson*
MRS. THEODOSIA ALSTON, *Burr's daughter*
NAPOLEON BONAPARTE, *First Consul of France*
TALLEYRAND, *Napoleon's Minister of Foreign Affairs*
MARBOIS, *Napoleon's Minister of Finance*
ALEXANDER HAMILTON, *Ex-Secretary of the Treasury of the United States*

⟪ Scenes

SCENE 1: The reception room adjoining Jefferson's private office in the White House, January, 1803.
SCENE 2: A sitting room in the Tuileries, Paris, France, April, 1803.

SCENE 3: Jefferson's private office in the White House, June, 1803.

❡ Settings

SCENE 1: A reception room adjoining the President's office in the White House. SCENE 2: A sitting room in the Tuileries, the royal palace of the former Kings of France in Paris, reflecting the gilded splendor of that period in its furnishings. SCENE 3: Jefferson's private office in the White House.

❡ Costumes

The trappers are dressed in fringed buckskins, moccasins and coonskin caps. They carry long-barreled rifles, hunting knives, shot pouches and powderhorns. Meriwether Lewis, Thomas Jefferson and James Monroe wear the new style introduced from Republican France: a cocked hat and a long-tailed coat, full-length tight trousers tucked into low boots; all in all, considerably more conservative than the colorful vests, coats, knee breeches, silk stockings, buckle-shoes and wigs worn at the end of the previous century. Aaron Burr wears the new vogue in clothing, but, in sharp contrast to Jefferson's conservative colors, his ensemble is colorful and highly adorned with braid and lace. Theodosia Alston elaborately gowned in the fashion of the English court: a wide flared skirt, tiny pointed bodice, low-cut neck, and a towering headdress. In SCENE 2, Napoleon, Talleyrand and Marbois are dressed in the same vogue as Burr—even more colorfully and highly trimmed with gold braid than he. In SCENE 3, Jefferson, Monroe and Hamilton are dressed as in Scene 1.

❡ Properties

SCENE 1: A conference table and several formal chairs, rug, paintings and portraits, small desk and chair, desk equipment and papers. SCENE 2: The furnishings are few, symbolizing the gilded age of the French monarchs; several mirrors on the wall, two or three chairs (Louis Sixteenth, if available), desk, lamps, rugs, etc. SCENE 3: A desk, secretary bookcase, three chairs, portrait of George Washington on the wall behind desk.

(Lighting

SCENE 1: Bright morning daylight. SCENE 2: Evening, the effect of lamp light. SCENE 3: Daylight entering from windows in rear wall, similar in architecture and placement to windows in Scene 1.

Scene I - "Louisiana"

Louisiana

SCENE 1

The reception room adjoining PRESIDENT THOMAS JEFFERSON's office in the White House, Washington, D.C., January, 1803. Bright morning sunlight streams in through the tall floor-length windows in the rear. A long conference table with several formal-looking chairs is in front of the windows. A beautiful rug lends a note of color and richness to the surroundings. Several portraits, with one of George Washington in a prominent position, hang on the walls. An entrance at the right leads to the corridor. An entrance at the left leads into the President's office. Just outside the office entrance is a desk and chair for MERIWETHER LEWIS, the President's secretary.

At curtain rise the room is unoccupied. A moment later, JEB DENBY enters from the right and very cautiously looks around. He motions to his two companions, who are as yet unseen, to follow him. BILL DAWSON and CHESTER COREY enter. The three single-file into the room—as woodsmen would—then stop to admire their surroundings. They remove their fur hats and tuck the tails under the broad belts that encircle their fringed buckskin jerkins. Shot pouches and powderhorns are suspended from a rawhide strap carried over their shoulders. Big hunting knives dangle from their belts. Their long-barreled rifles are crooked lovingly in their arms. They examine the room with pleased smiles and nods of approval. CHESTER is very intrigued with the rug, which he toes experimentally with his moccasin-shod foot. He pokes BILL to draw his attention to the rug.

CHESTER: Purty, ain't it, Bill?

(MERIWETHER LEWIS enters from the left. He looks

with dismay and astonishment at the three trappers,
then walks up to them.)

JEB (with an affable smile): How-do, mister. I'm Jeb Denby.
This be Bill Dawson . . . And this be Chester Corey.

CHESTER and BILL (together): How-do, sir.

LEWIS: Good morning, gentlemen. I'm Meriwether Lewis,
President Jefferson's secretary. May I assist you?

JEB: We just came up from Natchez way, and we got us a
mind to have us a talk with the President of these here
United States. Does he happen to be around, friend?

LEWIS (pleads, with a friendly smile): But, my dear sirs,
one can't just come in like this and expect to see the
President. (JEB turns to his companions with a puzzled
expression, then turns to LEWIS.)

JEB (inquiring politely): No? Why can't we?

LEWIS: Well . . . it just isn't done that way. (JEB turns again
to his companions. They shrug their shoulders in answer.)

JEB (agreeably): How do we get to see the President then,
my friend?

LEWIS: Well, sir . . . first you write to me . . . Then . . .

JEB (shakes his head negatively): Uh-uh. Can't do that.

LEWIS: Indeed? Why not, may I ask?

JEB: Can't write. (Turns to CHESTER) Can you, Chester?

CHESTER: Nary a hen scratch.

BILL (with pride): I can write my name . . . real good.

LEWIS (with sincere regret): I'm truly sorry, gentlemen . . .
(He steps back in alarm as CHESTER draws a big hunting knife from his sheath. CHESTER then begins to
whittle a chunk from a slab of chewing tobacco he has
taken from his pocket. He extends it to LEWIS.)

CHESTER: Chaw?

LEWIS (expelling his breath in relief): N-n-no, thank you.
(As CHESTER is about to pop the chunk in his mouth,
JEB speaks to him sternly.)

JEB: Put by your chaw tobacco, Chester. (CHESTER doesn't
understand why he should, but, with a shrug of incom-
prehension he stows it in his pocket. JEB turns to LEWIS,
speaks with some sharpness now.) Know where Natchez is,

178

my friend?

LEWIS: Yes, I do. In the Mississippi Territory. But . . .

JEB: Long way from Natchez to Washington, ain't it?

LEWIS: No doubt, sir . . .

JEB: Well, now . . . me and my two friends here, we made that long journey for to see Mr. Jefferson. (*Turns to the other two*) Right, boys?

CHESTER and BILL (*in unison*): Right, Jeb!

JEB: Right! (*To* LEWIS) And we come a long way, mister . . . a mighty long way . . . to tell Mr. Jefferson something we reckon it's important . . . mighty important for him to hear. Right, boys?

CHESTER and BILL (*in unison*): Right, Jeb!

JEB (*with quiet insistence*): So, Mr. Lewis, if Mr. Jefferson is in hollerin' distance, we'd be right obliged if you fetched him.

LEWIS (*pleads, as he motions toward the office door*): I'm quite sure you came to see him about something of great interest, sir, but at the moment he is in conference with Mr. Monroe on a matter of the utmost importance. I'd be very happy to arrange a meeting at his earliest convenience, if you would care to tell me what you wish to see him about.

(JEB *seems uncertain. He scratches his cheek as he looks to his companions for advice.*)

JEB: Don't know rightly if we should.

CHESTER: No, don't know rightly if we should, Jeb.

BILL: We came for to see Mr. Jefferson, and tell him private-like what we got to tell him.

LEWIS (*frowning*): But I'm his private secretary, and anything you have to say . . .

JEB: No offense meant, Mr. Lewis . . . 'Scuse us a minute.

(*He crooks his finger at the other two, summoning them for a conference. As* LEWIS *looks on, half-amused and half-annoyed, the three trappers rest the butts of their rifles on the floor, and, with their heads in a huddle, engage in whispered consultation. This continues as* JEFFERSON *and* MONROE *enter from the left.* JEFFERSON and MONROE *stop and regard the trappers with smiling interest.*)

LEWIS: These gentlemen, Mr. Jefferson, have just arrived from Natchez. They wish to see you, sir. I informed them . . .

(JEFFERSON *and* MONROE *respond with marked interest.*)

JEFFERSON: Natchez? (*He casts a knowing glance at* MONROE. *He walks up to the trappers with his hand outstretched.*) Welcome to Washington, gentlemen! You don't know how pleased I am to see you!

JEB (*beaming at* JEFFERSON's *warmth as he shakes his hand*): How-do, Mr. Jefferson. I'm Jeb Denby. (*Introducing his companions*) Chester Corey . . . Bill Dawson, sir.

JEFFERSON (*shaking hands*): Delighted to meet you, gentlemen. This is my friend Mr. James Monroe.

MONROE (*shaking hands all around*): It's a pleasure, gentlemen.

JEFFERSON: All the way up from Natchez to see me! What a long journey that must have been!

BILL (*grinning sheepishly*): A heap sight longer than it need have been, seein' as how we come by way of Philadelphy, Mr. Jefferson.

JEFFERSON (*surprised*): Philadelphia? But you came up from the south . . . ?

BILL: Aye, that we did. But the last we heard, the Capitol of these here U-nited States was staked out in Philadelphy.

JEFFERSON (*with a sympathetic laugh*): I'm terribly sorry. We moved the Capitol to Washington just short of two years ago.

JEB: Reckon news travels mighty slow before it gets to the backwoods, and the nation getting bigger and bigger all the time. (*With a glance at* LEWIS) Now, Mr. Jefferson, like I told your hired man here (JEFFERSON *and* MONROE *try to hide an amused smile as they glance at* LEWIS, *who is both amused and chagrined*) what we got to tell you we figure is mighty important. So, we beg your pardon, sir, for comin' in this way, 'thout a by-your-leave or such.

JEFFERSON (*firmly*): My good friend, there is certainly no

need to apologize, and no need to stand on ceremonies to see me! (*The trappers cannot resist casting a severe glance at* LEWIS.)

JEB: There's a heap of trouble brewin' down alongst the Mississippi, Mr. Jefferson. We thought to tell you about it, before things get out of hand.

JEFFERSON: Just what is the trouble, Mr. Denby?

JEB: It's about the taxes the Spanish are making us pay before we can land our rafts and unload our furs and such in New Orleans. You know, sir, there's a mighty sight of corn, tobacco and trappin's beginning to come down the Mississippi, and if we can't get 'em aboard the ships in New Orleans 'thout the Dons making us pay taxes, we just as lief chuck it all in the river, for all the good it will do us.

JEFFERSON (*very serious*): Yes, I have received reports about it. France has made them do that.

JEB (*puzzled*): The *Frenchies?* Don't Louisiana and New Orleans belong to the Spanish? Never had no trouble with *them*.

JEFFERSON (*with a grim smile*): A good question, Mr. Denby. (*Turning to* MONROE.) Is it not, Mr. Monroe?

MONROE: It is indeed. (*Looking inquiringly at* JEFFERSON.)

JEFFERSON (*nods*): You may as well tell them.

MONROE: You see, my friends . . . About two years ago, King Carlos of Spain signed a secret treaty with Napoleon, transferring all of the Louisiana Territory to France. It was quite secret, and there was never any official announcement or public ceremony to mark the event. Nothing was changed. New Orleans remained a free port as it was under Spanish rule. That is, until just recently.

CHESTER: Makes no matter *who* owns New Orleans now! The Frenchies or the Spanish! We just ain't goin' to pay them taxes!

BILL: No, sir! Ain't goin' to pay 'em! And if they keep askin' for it . . . we'll pay 'em! But not in gold or silver! We'll pay 'em in lead! Right, boys?

CHESTER: Right, Bill!

JEFFERSON (*smiling, but anxiously*): I hope you don't intend declaring war on Napoleon and France all on your own, do you?

BILL: Declare war? No, sir! But, when the Frenchies see the whole of the Mississippi Valley folk come pourin' into New Orleans, they sure 'nough will know it ain't no hand-kissin' party what's come a-callin'!

MONROE (*direfully*): And that, my friend, would be the worst possible thing you could do at this time. To involve us in a war with France, when we've hardly recovered from our struggle for independence from England . . . (*Shakes his head*)

JEB (*scratching his head in puzzlement*): But, you know, sir . . . there be some that are bent on stirrin' up trouble come what may.

MONROE (*with great interest*): Oh, indeed? (*He exchanges glances with* JEFFERSON.) Have you any idea who they are?

JEB: Not for sure, Mr. Monroe. But I'd bet a prime beaver skin against a jack-rabbit's that most of 'em are newcomers from east of the Allegheny. No, sir, can't figure rightly just who they are, but we know who they *ain't*. They ain't rivermen. They ain't trappers. They ain't farmers. And they ain't settlers. Right, boys?

BILL and CHESTER: Right, Jeb! They ain't!

JEFFERSON (*thoughtfully*): I see. (*Starts, apologetic*) But I'm being most ungracious. Please forgive me. Mr. Lewis, will you show the gentlemen into my office? See to their comfort and provide them with refreshments. (*To trappers.*) I'd like to talk further with you on this matter. Would you be so good as to wait for me? I'll be with you shortly.

JEB: Just as you say, Mr. Jefferson. (*As they exit into the office,* JEFFERSON *and* MONROE *look at each other in grim silence.*)

JEFFERSON: Well, James, it appears that your informant was quite right (*Smiling*) whoever he may have been.

MONROE: I'm sorry, Tom, I promised not to divulge his name.

JEFFERSON: Very well. But, nevertheless, we must act, and act quickly, before France takes formal possession of Louisiana. There would have been no problem—at least, no immediate problem—if the territory had remained in the hands of a weak nation like Spain. But, in the hands of Napoleon Bonaparte . . . (*Shakes his head*) Need I tell you what it may mean . . . in his mad drive for empire? (*He begins to pace the floor in thought.*)

MONROE: What can we do, Tom?

JEFFERSON: I must draw up instructions for Ambassador Livingston in Paris, and have it dispatched on the next vessel sailing for Europe. (*Stops pacing*) I will have him suggest to Napoleon how much we value the friendship of France and how we would like to continue our good relations. But, nevertheless, how unwise it would be for France to take possession of Louisiana without ceding New Orleans to us . . . or ceding some other suitable point at the mouth of the Mississippi River where we can land and ship our produce free of restrictions.

MONROE (*doubtfully*): That would sound almost like a threat, no matter how you put it. And to a vain man like Napoleon . . . ?

JEFFERSON (*with an innocent expression*): Threat? Why, not at all, James! Just a mere suggestion, that, if the war between France and Britain is renewed, there's a possibility that we, as a nation, may find ourselves involved and forced to marry ourselves to the British fleet . . . *if* trouble ensues along the Mississippi. And, if it does, who can foretell? France may not lose New Orleans, but the entire Louisiana Territory.

MONROE (*drily*): I see, just a mere suggestion. But I hope you are not forgetting, my friend, that Livingston will be dealing with two of the shrewdest minds in Europe. And I don't mean Napoleon for one.

JEFFERSON: Hmm, Yes. Talleyrand and Marbois. (*Giving it sober thought*) And as much as I admire and appreciate Livingston's abilities . . . (*He stops and looks at* MONROE *thoughtfully.*)

MONROE (*reading his mind, alarmed*): Oh, no, Tom! (*As* JEFFERSON *continues to regard him with a smile*) You know how I abhor sea voyages . . . how sick I get!

JEFFERSON: James, my good man, I hereby, as President of the United States of America, invest you with the title of Minister Plenipotentiary and Envoy Extraordinary to France!

MONROE (*with a scowl*): My friend . . . my dear friend Thomas Judas Jefferson.

JEFFERSON: Nonsense, James! Your good wife, Elizabeth, will bless me for it. The idea of a holiday abroad will just delight her.

MONROE (*with a resigned sigh*): You could talk an elephant into climbing a tree. (*Seriously, briskly*) Well, there's no time to be lost. (*Stands up*) I must inquire about sailings. (*He moves toward the exit right as* JEFFERSON *turns towards his office door left.*)

JEFFERSON (*turning*): James . . .

MONROE: Yes, Tom?

JEFFERSON: This mysterious informant of yours . . . did he have any idea who is behind this trouble along the Mississippi?

MONROE (*after a long pause*): Yes, Tom . . . some idea, but he wouldn't say who.

JEFFERSON: No definite proof, was that it?

MONROE (*nods*): No definite proof, that's it.

JEFFERSON: Hmm, that's what I thought.

    (*He waves a silent goodby and exits into his office.* MONROE *walks towards the door right. As* MONROE *just about reaches the door,* VICE-PRESIDENT AARON BURR *and his daughter* THEODOSIA *enter.* THEODOSIA *is richly and elaborately gowned. Her regal bearing has been so well developed and nurtured by her father, that, to all intents and purposes, it seems quite genuine and natural to her. Despite her haughty bearing,* THEODOSIA *is a very beautiful woman of twenty-two or so.* AARON BURR *is a dynamic, handsome man of forty-five, richly dressed, almost in defiance of* JEFFERSON'S *well known simplicity* of dress and manner.

BURR (*bowing to* MONROE): Good morning, Mr. Monroe.

MONROE (*bowing*): Good morning, Mr. Burr . . . Mrs. Alston.

THEODOSIA (*extending her hand*): How nice to see you, Mr. Monroe.

MONROE (*bowing over her hand*): My pleasure, madam.

BURR: Is the president in his office, Mr. Monroe?

MONROE (*as he watches* BURR's *expression closely*): Yes, three men from Natchez arrived to speak with him. (BURR *starts, but quickly recovers himself.*)

BURR: Shall we wait, Theo?

THEODOSIA: We may as well, father. I may not have the opportunity to see him for a considerable time to come.

BURR (*making light of it*): My daughter, sir, has quite a grievance to present to the president. She is simply devastated by Mr. Jefferson's decision to discontinue the weekly receptions in the White House.

MONROE: That is quite understandable, Mrs. Alston. Those weekly levees of his predecessor, Mr. Adams, must have been most enjoyable for the ladies.

THEODOSIA: My dear father, Mr. Monroe, makes it appear as if I, and I alone, were concerned, when I truly speak for all the ladies in Washington.

MONROE: My dear Mrs. Alston, if you indeed speak for all the ladies in Washington, then you speak in a voice powerful enough to penetrate to the very gates of heaven and cause St. Peter himself to tremble. (BURR *and* THEODOSIA *laugh.*)

THEODOSIA: Indeed, you overestimate us, sir.

MONROE: Not at all. I have good reason not to. (*Bows*) Now, if you will excuse me, madam . . . Mr. Burr.

BURR: Good day, Mr. Monroe.

THEODOSIA: Good day, sir. (MONROE *leaves, door right.*) He certainly is at home here in the White House, isn't he, father? (*With a curl of her lip*) One would think . . .

BURR (*resentfully*): Yes indeed, very much so. Even a choice suite for him and his wife whenever he has cause to come to Washington. Monroe is considered . . . (*Stops as* LEWIS *enters from* JEFFERSON's *office.* LEWIS *walks to his desk, waiting to receive them.* THEODOSIA *and* BURR *walk up to him.*)

LEWIS: Good morning, Mr. Burr.

BURR: Good morning, Mr. Lewis. (*To* THEODOSIA) Mr. Meriwether Lewis, my dear. President Jefferson's secretary. My daughter, Mrs. Alston, Mr. Lewis.

THEODOSIA (*assuming the right attitude, as far as she is concerned, to establish* LEWIS *at his proper social level*): I've had the pleasure, father.

LEWIS: My pleasure, madam.

THEODOSIA: I was introduced to Mr. Lewis at the President's levee a month or so ago.

LEWIS: Where we had a most engaging conversation.

THEODOSIA: Oh, did we, Mr. Lewis?

LEWIS: If you recall, you expressed considerable dismay at the conditions you found in Washington. I trust you have found some improvement since?

THEODOSIA: If there has been some, I'm afraid I've failed to notice it. If anything, the mud is deeper, the roads filthier, and its people more uncouth than ever.

BURR: Patience, Theo. After all, Rome wasn't built in a day, and Washington is barely two years old. Can't expect perfection in so short a time.

THEODOSIA (*sarcastic*): How true, father. Really, all Washington needs is houses, roads, well-informed men, some amiable women . . . and other such trifles.

LEWIS (*with hardly perceptible sarcasm, bows*): At least we are acquiring the amiable women, madam. (BURR *eyes him narrowly, detecting the sarcasm which is lost on* THEODOSIA. *She condescends to smile in appreciation of the compliment.*)

THEODOSIA: And also gallants, I see. But do tell me, Mr. Lewis . . . why did they remove the capital from New York? A civilized metropolis of forty thousand souls! First New York, then Philadelphia, now Washington. Heavens above, need the capital of a nation be shunted about from place to place like a lady's bandbox? And if they did have to move the government again, how, in heaven's name, did they fasten upon this muddy, mosquito-ridden swamp?

LEWIS: Because of its central position between the northern and southern states, Mrs. Alston.

THEODOSIA (*pretending innocence*): Oh, was *that* the reason? Dear me, how unjust people can be! They say . . . because General Washington was Virginian, and likewise Mr. Jefferson . . .

BURR (*frowning, feeling that she is carrying it too far*): Oh, come, come, Theo!

THEODOSIA (*with a laugh, to cover her malice*): And it has just occurred to me, Mr. Lewis . . . are you not, too, a Virginian?

LEWIS: You flatter me, madam.

THEODOSIA (*with a lift of her eyebrow*): Oh?

LEWIS: Yes, indeed. To think that I, a humble civil servant, may have helped determine where the capital of a nation would be. (BURR and THEODOSIA *laugh at this, then* BURR *shows a little impatience.*)

BURR: Will the President be engaged for much longer?

LEWIS: 'Tis hard to say, sir. I do know, though, he has a very busy schedule this morning.

THEODOSIA: Certainly not too busy that he can't find time for the Vice-President and his daughter, sir? (LEWIS, *at a loss, looks at* BURR. THEODOSIA'S *glance at* BURR *is a prod.*)

BURR (*coolly*): Will you be good enough to inform the President that we wait upon his pleasure, Mr. Lewis?

LEWIS (*bows with a touch of stiffness*): Certainly, Mr. Burr. (LEWIS *exits into* JEFFERSON'S *office.*)

THEODOSIA (*resentfully*): To have to grovel before an underling to see the great Mr. Jefferson! Oh, to think, father . . . to think, were it not for that treacherous wretch Alexander Hamilton (*Points towards office*) you would be sitting in there now, not that bumbling dilettante, who is far better suited to be the president of a university than president of a nation. The great leveler indeed! He would drag every true gentleman down to the level of each sniveling, tobacco-drooling clod . . . and call it democracy!

BURR: We must learn to be good gamblers, Theo . . . to accept our losses and continue to play for . . . aye, greater gains.

THEODOSIA (indicating surroundings): What can we possibly gain that is greater than this?

BURR (scornfully): This? This represents a mere principality, a province, compared to the vast empire that lies to the west.

THEODOSIA (with an enthralled look): Louisiana!

BURR: Louisiana? That, my dear child, is only the beginning, a stepping stone on the path to a golden empire greater in size, greater in wealth than the combined conquests of Caesar, Alexander and Kubla Khan! (Pauses, then lower) Mexico!

(While THEODOSIA is lost in his dream, BURR turns aside.)

THEODOSIA (her eyes glittering, low): Mexico!

BURR (with a twist of his wrists): But first . . . to break this rabble-ridden nation into two warring segments: North and South, clutching at each other's throats; so shattered and torn with bloody strife, that, even if they willed, they couldn't stop me from founding a dynasty that will live forever! (He turns to THEODOSIA and grasps her wrists.) And all . . . all for you, my beautiful child. Yes, it was for this . . . and with this in mind, that I groomed you from childhood. Taught you how to speak, how to stand, how to walk and hold up your head like a princess, to grace the court of an emperor!

THEODOSIA (coming out of her spell): Father . . . father, if I didn't know you I would say you were mad! Mad!

BURR (releasing her and turning away with a short laugh): Mad? No . . . A dreamer? . . . Perhaps. But one who knows how to turn a dream into a living reality.

THEODOSIA: But, when?

BURR: Oh, not too long. The wheels are turning; and when I am elected Governor of New York, they will begin to spin faster, and faster, and . . . (Stops as JEFFERSON's door

opens and the three trappers step out followed by JEFFER-
SON and LEWIS. BURR and THEODOSIA eye the trappers;
BURR with narrowed eyes, THEODOSIA with distaste. JEF-
FERSON is talking as he appears.)
JEFFERSON: . . . And tell your neighbors in the Valley not
to do anything rash. I'm sure the whole situation will be
resolved to everyone's satisfaction, given time. (Shaking
hands) Goodby, and thank you again for coming all this
way to speak with me. You have been most helpful.
TRAPPERS: Goodby, Mr. Jefferson . . . Goodby.
JEB: We hope you can get down Natchez way sometime, Mr.
Jefferson. We'd do you mighty proud if you did. Right,
boys?
BILL: Right, Jeb!
  (CHESTER doesn't answer. In absolute fascination, his
  eyes are riveted on THEODOSIA's hair-do. The three
  trappers walk to the exit. BURR and THEODOSIA walk
  toward JEFFERSON with smiles, that, peculiarly enough,
  resemble each other's. CHESTER trails behind his companions, his eyes still glued to THEODOSIA's hair. Just
  before they reach the door, which is being held open by
  LEWIS, CHESTER speaks up.)
CHESTER (low, but quite audible to all): Lawdy, Billy boy,
  wouldn't a Shawnee Injun just love to get his paws on
  that scalp! (THEODOSIA's smile freezes on her face. She
  turns her head to glare at Chester. JEFFERSON finds it
  hard to control a smile. LEWIS, at the door, can't stifle one
  explosive "Haw!" before his face blanks out quickly.)
JEB (sharply out of the corner of his mouth): Hobble your
  lip, you big lummox!
JEFFERSON (bowing): Mrs. Alston . . . Mr. Burr . . . do come
  in.

SCENE 2

A sitting room in the Tuileries, the royal palace of the former
kings of France, occupied by NAPOLEON BONAPARTE as his
Paris residence. It is April, 1803. Several gilded mirrors hang

on the walls. *The chairs and desks are of the period of the previous, and ill-fated, monarch, Louis the Sixteenth.*

At curtain rise NAPOLEON *is striding back and forth across the floor with his hands clasped behind him. He is in one of his dark, impatient moods.* TALLEYRAND, *his Minister of Foreign Affairs, is standing at a respectful distance.*

NAPOLEON: I should have crushed those curséd English when I had all Europe beaten and down on its knees begging for mercy! (*Stops to point an accusing finger at* TALLEYRAND) But, no! I had to listen to you, Talleyrand, my brilliant Minister of Foreign Affairs, and others like you who advised me to sign that truce at Amiens! (*With a wave of his hand.*) Now look at them. Bending every effort to strengthen their fleets and build up their military again! I demand of you, Talleyrand, how long will they bide their time before they decide to attack France? Next year? Next month? Next week?

TALLEYRAND: They are far from ready to start the war again, General Bonaparte.

NAPOLEON (*scathingly*): And we should just sit here and wait for the day they are ready, yes? . . . No! (*Taps his chest*) Napoleon Bonaparte does not wait to be attacked! Napoleon attacks first! Yes, I will invade England and carry the war to their own soil this time!

TALLEYRAND: No one has been able to invade England since William the Conqueror in 1066.

NAPOLEON (*snaps*): Thank you! Thank you for the history lesson. Talleyrand, if I didn't know my history, I wouldn't be making history. And I will continue to make history when I land my troops in England and show them how it feels to be under the heel of a conqueror for a change. (*Starts pacing again*) That contemptible nation of shopkeepers! So snugly secure behind their watery fortress all these centuries, while their armies, time and time again, overrun the continent to turn the soil of France into a bloody quagmire as their people sit at home, swilling their abominable ale and stuffing their big bellies with their foul-smelling mutton joints! (*Shudders with repugnance at the thought*) Uhh! . . . while all Europe starved. (*He stops to stare at the floor with his head thrust forward. Then he straightens up and strikes his fist into his palm.*) But I need ships! Warships! Transports! And that takes gold . . . gold. (*Scowling at* TALLEYRAND) Perhaps you, monsieur, can tell me where I can find the gold to build those ships?

TALLEYRAND (*with a contemptuous curl of his lip*): May I suggest that you ask that of your Minister of Finance, Barbe-Marbois? I'm sure he can tell you where there is plenty of gold.

NAPOLEON (*angrily*): Don't trifle with me, monsieur!

TALLEYRAND: Your pardon, my general, but I do not trifle. (*With a sardonic smile he points his finger at the floor.*) There is all the gold you would need right here in France. Buried in the ground under haystacks and manure piles. Hidden away in chests under beds in many a sleeping chamber. Cemented into the walls of many a chateau in the provinces, where it was all quickly concealed when your esteemed wizard of finance, Monsieur Marbois, decided to print paper money.

NAPOLEON (*as he begins to pace again*): Bah!

TALLEYRAND: What in the name of God did he expect? That our most practical people would rush to exchange their beautiful gold coins for paper money . . . paper money of doubtful value? If you recall, I strongly advised . . .

NAPOLEON (*stopping him short*): Yes, yes! So you were right! (*Scowling at him, grudgingly*) But have I not always expressed my deepest admiration for your talents, my dear Talleyrand? (*With a quick change of mood and a cryptic smile*) Especially your great talent for always finding yourself on the winning side in every major change that has overtaken France in the past twenty years? (*Chuckles*) But always!

TALLEYRAND (*murmurs*): I but always seek to serve my beloved France, monsieur.

NAPOLEON (*cryptically*): Such patriotic zeal is most commendable, my dear Talleyrand.

TALLEYRAND: Whosoever is master in France, him will I serve.

NAPOLEON: But of course! (*Chuckles*) You served His Holiness, Pope Pius the Sixth, and he made you Bishop of Autun . . .

TALLEYRAND (*intones*): In the year of Our Lord, 1789.

NAPOLEON: And two years later, after the storming of the Bastille and the success of the Revolution, voila! . . . we find you President of the National Assembly. (*With a mockingly exalted flourish*) Citoyen Talleyrand! Hah! And most insistent in demanding that church property be confiscated by the State.

TALLEYRAND (*sighs with mock regret*): For which I was most justly excommunicated by His Holiness in Rome.

NAPOLEON (*quizzically*): But then . . . then suddenly (*With a gesture of inquiry*) you leave France. What happened, my loyal son of France?

TALLEYRAND (*with a shrug*): Under the conditions that prevailed, I felt there was no opportunity for my talents to be fully employed or appreciated . . . shall I say?

NAPOLEON: So? Or did you sense that the Revolution was bound for failure, due to the excesses of its leaders? (*Sweeps his finger across his throat*) Or, perhaps, you didn't care to accommodate Dr. Guillotin's pretty little invention and have your head fall into the same basket that received Robespierre's?

TALLEYRAND (*with a sad sigh*): It is to regret, monsieur, but snobbery has always remained one of my most deplorable faults. Furthermore, I'm particularly fond of this head of mine and would regret parting with it under any circumstances.

NAPOLEON (*chuckles*): Talleyrand, you are one in a million!

TALLEYRAND (*bowing in acknowledgment*): Thank you, monsieur.

NAPOLEON: And so, when the spirit of the Revolution was dead . . .

TALLEYRAND: Your pardon, monsieur . . . It might be more

correct to say . . . when all its *leaders* were dead. So like a tragedy by that English playwright, William Shakespeare, who oft eliminated by sword, dagger, poison, and all manner of means, every major character in the cast, and then, for a total lack of players to continue with the performance, he had no choice but to bring down the final curtain. Finis!

NAPOLEON: Five years you remained away, in England and the United States. What brought you back?

TALLEYRAND (*with his shrewd smile*): Perhaps, monsieur, to serve the future monarch of France . . . Napoleon Bonaparte.

NAPOLEON (*pauses for a long time to scowl at him, but one can see that he is not too displeased at* TALLEYRAND's *presumptuousness*): So . . . you would have me a king, would you?

TALLEYRAND: A king? But no, monsieur. That you are already. Certainly in fact, if not in title. All you lack is a crown to make it official. No, I would not have you a king. Much too common a product in Europe. So common indeed, that the people think nothing of seeing them come, or seeing them go. A dispensable and expendable product. And that is bad. Very bad. For, when people, with placidity, begin to accept the idea that a thing is not meant to be permanent, they are too prone to shorten its life span and consign it to an early grave before its time has fully run; be it a man, an idea . . . or a king. (NAPOLEON *is following him very closely, although he chooses to play it as* TALLEYRAND *does—lightly.*)

NAPOLEON: What, no crown, Monsieur Talleyrand? I am devastated with disappointment!

TALLEYRAND: Ah, forgive me, monsieur! It was not my intent to deprive you of a crown. On the contrary, I would fashion you a crown that befits the role you are destined to play . . . as the Emperor Napoleon of France. (*There is a long silence as they regard each other;* TALLEYRAND, *with a smile, reading* NAPOLEON's *thoughts behind that deep concentrated frown.*)

NAPOLEON (scowling): And, I presume, you have already chosen the role you will play in that empire, my dear Talleyrand?

TALLEYRAND (without hesitation, but with assumed flippancy): But of course! Your Grand Chamberlain—(Inviting him to try it on for size)—Sire. (A rapid transition of multiple feelings is evident in NAPOLEON's change of expression: his glare changes to a glimmer of admiration, then a chuckle into a laugh as he slaps his thigh.)

NAPOLEON: Talleyrand, you are magnificent! Magnificent! (MARBOIS enters from door left. He holds a number of papers in his hand. He bows to NAPOLEON, ignoring TALLEYRAND, who regards him with cool contempt. NAPOLEON is irritated at being interrupted. He has been enjoying himself immensely, and been given ideas to feed his ambitious dreams.)

NAPOLEON: Yes, yes, Marbois, what is it?

MARBOIS: General Bonaparte, I find myself in a position to report to you . . .

NAPOLEON (impatiently): For the love of God, Marbois, when will you ever learn to report without that ridiculous preamble! Say what you have to say and be done with it! (MARBOIS is put out of countenance as he bows. TALLEYRAND's face wears a malicious smile of satisfaction at MARBOIS' discomfiture.)

MARBOIS: Your pardon, general. (Rattles it off) The American Ambassador, Monsieur Livingston, and Monsieur James Monroe, Minister Plenipotentiary and Envoy Extraordinary to France—(NAPOLEON casts his eyes up to heaven)—wish to arrange for the purchase of the City of New Orleans in America from the Government of France.

NAPOLEON (with a quick, eager response, demands): How much?

TALLEYRAND (startled): What?

MARBOIS (off balance for the moment): Eh?

NAPOLEON (irritated, impatient): How much? How much will they pay?

MARBOIS (with a shrug and a gesture of doubt): It is hard

to say, general. They are very shrewd bargainers, these Yankees.

NAPOLEON (*throwing up his hands in despair, longingly*): Oh, if only Rosa Bonafaccio were here to handle this for me!

MARBOIS: Rosa Bona . . . Bonafaccio? Who, if I may make bold to inquire, is . . . ?

NAPOLEON: Rosa Bonafaccio—a Corsican fishwife I knew as a lad in the town of Ajaccio where I was born. By the saints! Your American gentlemen would be lucky to go home wearing their breeches if she were here to handle this deal for me!

MARBOIS: (*murmurs*): They did hint they might pay two million dollars . . .

NAPOLEON (*annoyed*): Dollars? How much is that in civilized money, Marbois? (*Turning to* TALLEYRAND.) Remind me, Talleyrand . . . the first thing I must do when I have finished with England, is to do away with all this stupid business of pounds, dollars, kronen, guilder . . . or what have you. Francs! Everything in the entire world will be reckoned in francs! (MARBOIS, *frowning in deep concentration, has been doing some mental arithmetic.*)

MARBOIS: Two millions of dollars come to about ten million francs, general.

NAPOLEON (*scowling*): Is that all? Not enough! It might build me five . . . six ships at the most, and I need at the least forty!

TALLEYRAND: Surely, general, you aren't seriously thinking of selling New Orleans?

NAPOLEON (*demands*): And why not?

TALLEYRAND: But, monsieur! New Orleans! Whoever controls New Orleans controls the whole Mississippi River and the Louisiana Territory. Mon Dieu, you give away New Orleans and you may as well part with *all* of Louisiana!

(NAPOLEON *stops short in his pacing and, after one quick moment of thought, strikes his palms together in decision. He swings around to face* TALLEYRAND.)

LOUISIANA

NAPOLEON: Now, *that* is a thought! The first sensible thing I've heard all day!

TALLEYRAND (*appalled*): Surely, you're not serious, general?

NAPOLEON: Serious? What need have we for that wilderness?

TALLEYRAND: It has tremendous potential. I spent three years in the United States, and I know there is an empire to be built there. (*Pointedly*) Not alone Louisiana, general . . . but Mexico . . . Mexico.

NAPOLEON: Talleyrand, you should know by this time that the colonies across the sea are hard to hold. We lost Canada to the English. And we just had two armies wiped out in Santo Domingo; one by pestilence, and the other by that devil, Toussaint L'Overture, and his black demons.

MARBOIS (*gravely*): A most expensive campaign, general. We almost drained our treasury in that unfortunate venture.

NAPOLEON (*bitterly*): Need I be reminded of that, Marbois?

MARBOIS (*murmurs*): Your pardon, general.

NAPOLEON: No, Talleyrand, America does not interest me any more. Furthermore, when we find ourselves at war with England again, don't you think the Americans will *take* Louisiana?

TALLEYRAND: They wouldn't dare risk a war with France!

NAPOLEON (*scornfully*): Wouldn't they though? Talleyrand, sometimes I wonder if you truly deserve the reputation of being the most cunning mind in all of Europe. I tell you, not only will they take Louisiana and pay us not a sou, but they will ally themselves with England to gain the protection of their fleet. (*Swings on* MARBOIS) Marbois, do you agree?

MARBOIS: I am *entirely* in accord with you, general.

NAPOLEON: Very well then! Deal with these gentlemen and get what you can. Seventy . . . eighty million francs. As long as it is enough to build thirty or forty vessels. Give what you will. New Orleans, or all Louisiana. (*Wags a finger at him*) But in gold, Marbois, in gold!

MARBOIS: It shall be as you wish, general.

TALLEYRAND: Monsieur, I appeal to you to consider . . .

NAPOLEON: Be quiet, Talleyrand! I have made my decision,

and I don't care to hear another word on this matter. (*He notes* TALLEYRAND's *chagrin at having his opinion disregarded in such a blunt manner; he tries to make some amends, using a softer tone.*) Talleyrand, Talleyrand, what are a few million miles of wilderness compared to the possession of England? (TALLEYRAND *does not answer, knowing full well how futile it is to try to change* NAPOLEON's *mind once he has arrived at a decision.* NAPOLEON, *somewhat peeved at* TALLEYRAND's *cold silence, turns to* MARBOIS *sharply.*) Marbois, you know my wishes.

MARBOIS: You have but to command, General Bonaparte.

NAPOLEON: Good! And I want no delay. Good day, messieurs. (*He turns and exits door right.* MARBOIS *looks at* TALLEYRAND *with a triumphant smirk, pleased to note the cold rage that* TALLEYRAND *is repressing.*)

MARBOIS: Monsieur, how can you question Napoleon's judgment in this matter?

TALLEYRAND: As Minister of Foreign Affairs, it is my responsibility to weigh the cost and consequences of any act that involves a treaty with another nation.

MARBOIS: As it is my responsibility, as Minister of Finance, to enhance the nation's treasury and balance its books.

TALLEYRAND: Spoken like a petty-bourgeois shopkeeper, monsieur.

MARBOIS (*resentfully*): You are being most offensive, monsieur!

TALLEYRAND: But am I not always, monsieur? (MARBOIS *is about to retort, but turns angrily away and starts for the door.*)

MARBOIS: Bah, you waste my time, while I have important business to transact with those two American gentlemen.

TALLEYRAND: Which I'm sure you will handle in a manner that might do credit to a Corsican fishwife . . . (*As* MARBOIS *swings around to face him, his face tense with rage*) . . . considering your origin, Monsieur Marbois. (MARBOIS *steps toward* TALLEYRAND.)

MARBOIS (*choking with rage*): Why, you . . . you . . .

TALLEYRAND (*with a cold smile wags his finger at him*

warningly): Ah-ah, careful, Marbois . . . careful. I understand you are much more adept with a pen in your hand
than you are with a dueling sword.
(MARBOIS represses his rage, turns away and walks to
the door. TALLEYRAND watches him go, a satisfied, dis-
dainful smile on his face.)

SCENE 3

JEFFERSON's office in the White House. The furnishings reflect the simple good taste of JEFFERSON. A large desk and
chair down center, facing front. A rich rug on the floor. Two
or three more chairs near the desk. A secretary bookcase up
right center. To the left of the bookcase a door right leads
into the reception room. A door, left third entrance, leads
to other rooms in the White House. Daylight enters from
the floor-length windows in the back wall which are of the
same placement and architectural design as in the reception
room.
At curtain rise JAMES MONROE, holding a portfolio in his
hand, is being welcomed by JEFFERSON.
JEFFERSON (warmly shaking his hand and embracing his
shoulder): My dear friend, how good it is to see you home
again!
MONROE (with a tired sigh as he sits down): And how good
it feels to be back home again.
JEFFERSON (concerned): You do look tired. Was it a rough
journey?
MONROE: Thomas, there were moments when I feared I
would never see the blessed shore again. Oh, not that I
cared . . . I was that seasick. Indeed, it would have been
a relief to depart this life and so end my misery.
JEFFERSON (laughing): Oh, come now, James, surely it
wasn't as bad as all that!
MONROE (scowling): No? I'll have you know I even com-
posed an epitaph to be engraved on a memorial to be
erected in my honor. (With mock solemnity) "In memory
of James Monroe, who gave his all to his beloved country

... including his breakfast, lunches and dinners." (JEFFER-
SON *laughs.*)

JEFFERSON: And Elizabeth, how did she fare?

MONROE (*in utter disbelief*): Elizabeth? She enjoyed it!
Truly enjoyed it! (*With a wondering shake of his head*)
Can you credit that, Tom?

JEFFERSON: Just a better man than you, James.

MONROE (*with a serious change of tone*): You received my
dispatch from Paris? (*He begins to open his portfolio.*)

JEFFERSON (*sitting down*): I did indeed! About a fortnight
ago. Congratulations, James! What a magnificent diplo-
matic maneuver to achieve such results!

MONROE (*murmurs with some uneasiness*): Ah yes . . . yes,
indeed . . . quite. (*He extracts a document from his
portfolio.*)

JEFFERSON (*rising quickly to pace the floor*): But how am I
going to present the matter to Congress? (*With a rueful
laugh*) To hand them a fait accompli . . . ?

MONROE (*soberly*): A good question, my friend, a very good
question. (*He deposits the document on the desk.*)

JEFFERSON: I've searched my soul, and every clause in our
glorious Constitution. (*Stops to look down at* MONROE)
And, you know, James, I can't for the life of me find a
single word which gives me the power as president to
buy (*Points to document*) . . . why, even the foolscap
that document is written on, without prior consent from
Congress. And here I've gone ahead and bought an entire
city! New Orleans!

MONROE (*finding it difficult to break the news*): Tom . . .
we didn't buy just New Orleans . . . (JEFFERSON *is so
absorbed in his problem he doesn't hear* MONROE *finish.*)
We bought the entire Louisiana Territory.

JEFFERSON: Yes, but isn't it just wonderful . . . (*Does a
double-take*) We did . . . what!?

MONROE (*blurts it out*): I said we bought all of the Louisiana Territory. The whole kit and kaboodle! (JEFFERSON
just stares at him; then sinks into a chair, looking at
MONROE *and not quite believing his ears.* MONROE *finishes*

weakly.) For . . . for fifteen million dollars. (JEFFERSON *places his palm over his eyes and begins to chuckle*.)
JEFFERSON: Oh, my, oh my, oh, my! All . . .
MONROE: I'm sorry, Tom, I just couldn't turn it down! Why, it's the biggest bargain since Jehovah deeded the Garden of Eden to Adam! It all came about after I sent you my last dispatch. There wasn't time to consult with you, so I took it upon myself. It would have taken months to send you a message and receive a reply in return. I had to act quickly. For, you know Napoleon. He's as changeable as the wind. And . . .
JEFFERSON (*rises to his feet in excitement to shake* MONROE's *shoulder*): But it's wonderful, James, wonderful! To double the size of our nation in one fell swoop! (*He picks up the treaty from the desk; looks at it anxiously*.) James . . . are you sure? (MONROE *is considerably relieved by* JEFFERSON's *enthusiastic response*.)
MONROE (*beaming*): All signed, sealed, and ready for delivery, Tom. All it needs is your signature, and Louisiana is ours.
JEFFERSON (*wryly*): I wish it were as simple as all that.
MONROE: Hmmm . . . yes, Congress.
JEFFERSON (*sighs*): But, we may just as well be killed for a sheep as be killed for a lamb. Nevertheless, I dread to think what the Federalists will do; what they will say.
MONROE (*drily*): The Federalists in Congress will do and say what Alexander Hamilton tells them to do and say . . . you know that.
JEFFERSON: Yes, it will all depend upon Alexander Hamilton, my most bitter political enemy. What chance have I to receive his cooperation when I'm giving him such a prime opportunity to make political capital for his party?
MONROE: That is why I made that stopover in New York, Tom . . . to see him before the matter was made public.
JEFFERSON: Good! Very wise of you, James. And . . . ?
MONROE: I was able to induce him to journey with me to Washington.
JEFFERSON: He's here, now?

MONROE: Yes. In fact, he's in my chambers waiting for an invitation to see you any time you are ready to receive him.

JEFFERSON: I'll be delighted to receive him, and that, immediately! (*Walking to door right*) This is one matter that cannot wait. (*He opens the door and speaks to* LEWIS.) Mr. Lewis . . .

LEWIS (*voice, offstage*): Yes, Mr. Jefferson?

JEFFERSON: Mr. Hamilton is in Mr. Monroe's chambers. Will you present my respects and ask him to do me the honor to come to my office?

LEWIS: Certainly, sir. (JEFFERSON *walks back to* MONROE, *looking very thoughtful.*)

MONROE (*wondering*): But, can we trust him not to abuse your confidence . . . turn it to his advantage?

JEFFERSON (*after giving it considerable thought*): Yes. I would say, in this matter, yes, we can trust him.

MONROE (*looking doubtful*): Hmm . . .

JEFFERSON (*speaking slowly*): James . . . Alexander Hamilton is scrupulously honest . . . That is, in his personal life.

MONROE (*skeptically*): And how about his political life?

JEFFERSON (*with a wry smile and a shake of his head*): As corrupt as can be, I'm afraid.

MONROE: I don't see how it is possible for one to divide oneself so. Either a man is completely honest in all things, or . . .

JEFFERSON: Perhaps I didn't make myself clear.

MONROE (*murmurs*): Afraid you didn't.

JEFFERSON: James, when Hamilton and I served in General Washington's cabinet when he was President, Hamilton as Secretary of the Treasury, and I as Secretary of State, we differed strongly on practically all basic issues.

MONROE (*with a grin*): Now that's putting it mildly, from all I hear.

JEFFERSON (*laughs*): Yes, we did have a rather stormy time together, didn't we? I recall, as if it were but yesterday, Washington standing at a distance, frowning anxiously while listening to Alexander and me going at each other

over some matter or another . . . I forget now what it was
. . . until he couldn't bear it any longer. We heard the
general cry, "Ye gods! How I long for the peaceful boom-
ing of cannon and the rattle of musketry at the Battle
of Brooklyn Heights!" (*They laugh.*) Yes, indeed, we did
have some glorious battles, Alex and I. (*With sad reminiscence*) Alex . . . (*With a change of tone*) But never
once did I ever doubt that what he proposed was in his
own mind, at least, for the good of the country. Unfortu-
nately, he would use every means, fair or foul, to have his
way, whether it was in violation of the Constitution and
the law of the land or no. For he believed that the Constitution was only a temporary measure, and should be
applied with all flexibility if circumstances demand it.
(*Thoughtfully*) Yes, James, Hamilton is honest as a man,
but, as a politician, believing as he does in the necessity
of either force or corruption to govern men, he will stop
at nothing, for he has no faith in man's ability to govern
himself. (*Shakes his head*) And if men cannot be trusted
to govern themselves, how can they trust others to govern
them?

MONROE (*sighs*): How true, my friend, how true.

JEFFERSON (*smiles in reminiscence*): I recall so well meeting
with him in President Washington's home in Mt. Vernon.
The room where we met contained a collection of portraits
of remarkable men. Among them were those of Bacon,
Newton, and Locke. Hamilton asked me who they were.
I told him they were my trinity of the three greatest men
the world had ever produced. I named them for him. I
recall how he paused, then said: "The greatest man that
ever lived was Julius Caesar."

MONROE (*dourly*): Yes, he would think so. (LEWIS *appears
at door right.*)

LEWIS: Mr. Alexander Hamilton, sir.

(JEFFERSON *steps forward as* ALEXANDER HAMILTON *appears in doorway.* HAMILTON, *the man, is ambitious,
generous, devoted, proud, quick to take offense and quick
to forgive, of flashing mind and inexhaustible energy. He*

possesses great personal charm and attractiveness. With his reddish-brown hair, bright brown eyes, fine forehead, and firm mouth and chin, he is exceptionally handsome, pleasant when he talks, severe and thoughtful when at work. He loves efficiency, order and organization. He is a man of action, as compared to JEFFERSON, the man of thought and philosophical idealism; two men, who, by their very nature, were bound to rub each other the wrong way. HAMILTON steps forward to meet JEFFERSON with a bow.)

HAMILTON: Mr. Jefferson.

JEFFERSON (extending his hand): Mr. Hamilton, how kind of you to make that long, tiresome journey from New York to meet with me!

HAMILTON: By no means tiresome. (With a bow in MONROE's direction) I couldn't have wished for a more engaging companion on the journey.

MONROE (with a bow): The pleasure was all mine, Mr. Hamilton.

JEFFERSON: Do sit down, won't you? (HAMILTON sits down. JEFFERSON sits near him, avoiding the President's chair behind the desk. MONROE finds a seat close to the desk.)

HAMILTON (briskly): Now, sir, if there is any way I can be of assistance, you may account me completely at your service.

JEFFERSON (smiles): You always did like to get down to business as quickly as possible, didn't you?

HAMILTON (affably). Oh, I didn't mean to hasten you.

JEFFERSON: I'm sure it was not your intention to do so. But, in truth, this matter brooks no delay. (Picks up the treaty from the desk) I understand Mr. Monroe did discuss this treaty with you.

HAMILTON: He did, but only broadly. I did not read it.

JEFFERSON (with a laugh): I must confess, I, myself have not read it.

MONROE (takes another copy from his portfolio): I have another draft here; unsigned, but a fair copy in all other respects.

HAMILTON (*with a smile and a quizzical lift of his brow*): Oh, the treaty has already been signed, Mr. Monroe?

MONROE (*uncomfortable, clearing his throat*): By Marbois for the Government of France, and Mr. Livingston and myself for the Government of the United States.

HAMILTON: Indeed? (*Looks at* JEFFERSON *with a twinkle in his eye*) Then all it needs is your signature, Mr. President, and the Louisiana Territory is ours.

JEFFERSON: Is it as simple as all that, Mr. Hamilton?

HAMILTON (*innocently*): And why not, I pray you?

JEFFERSON: Candidly, I question if I have the right under the Constitution to do so.

HAMILTON (*looking down at the treaty which* MONROE *hands him; with a sardonic smile*): Ah, yes, the Constitution. (*Looking up at* JEFFERSON) And there are no other questions which might deter you, Mr. Jefferson?

JEFFERSON: Such as . . ?

HAMILTON: Such as . . . has Napoleon the legal right under the French Constitution to sell Louisiana? (JEFFERSON, *with an embarrassed grin, looks down at the floor and remains silent.*) Or daren't you ask yourself that question, Mr. Jefferson?

JEFFERSON (*with a wry laugh*): I suppose there are times when it doesn't do for one to ask too many questions . . . or nothing would ever be accomplished.

HAMILTON (*murmurs, with an amused, gentle dig*): Hear! Hear! Is that Thomas Jefferson talking? Or is it the voice of Alexander Hamilton we hear?

JEFFERSON (*with a grin, murmurs*): Touché! (MONROE *has been following their conversation with considerable annoyance and impatience.*)

MONROE (*scowling*): What's this about the French Constitution, Mr. Hamilton?

HAMILTON (*with amusement, as he looks at* JEFFERSON): Ah, here I must defer to our learnéd president. For, is he not accounted by all a renowned scholar of constitutional law?

JEFFERSON (*looking at* HAMILTON *with a slight smile as he rubs his cheek*): What Mr. Hamilton no doubt refers to, James, is an article in the French Constitution which forbids the alienation of French territory under any circumstances.

MONROE (*glowering at* HAMILTON): Hang it all, Tom, I always did say, stay away from lawyers! They only complicate matters! Do more harm than good! (JEFFERSON *and* HAMILTON *laugh.*)

JEFFERSON: And that from a colleague?

HAMILTON: Forgive me, sir, if I further complicate matters by questioning if Louisiana rightfully belongs to France?

JEFFERSON (*frowning*): I must confess, I don't follow you there, Mr. Hamilton. The King of Spain *did* cede Louisiana to France by treaty, did he not?

HAMILTON: Ah, yes, indeed he did. But, has France, as yet, fulfilled the conditions as required of that treaty? (MONROE *looks blank;* JEFFERSON's *face wears an embarrassed grin again.*) Ah, I see you know what I'm talking about, Mr. Jefferson.

JEFFERSON (*nods*): I believe I do.

MONROE (*explodes*): Well, I don't! And I'd appreciate . . .

JEFFERSON (*holding up his hand*): James, when the King of Spain ceded the Louisiana Territory to Napoleon, the treaty stipulated that France would never cede the Territory to any other power, and if France did not occupy it, she would cede the Territory back to Spain. (MONROE *is heard to growl.*) Is that what you had in mind, Mr. Hamilton?

HAMILTON (*grins*): I see you have searched deep, Mr. Jefferson, to determine whether or not the seller holds clear title to the property being offered for sale.

JEFFERSON: And I see that you don't intend making things easy for me, Mr. Hamilton.

HAMILTON (*protests, with a mischievous smile*): Not at all, Mr. Jefferson! It's merely that, as an attorney, I always have the interests of my client at heart. If I may be bold enough to account you as my client at this moment?

JEFFERSON (*bows with a smile*): You may indeed, Mr.

LOUISIANA

Hamilton. And might I say, I couldn't hope for a more competent lawyer to advise me at this moment. (MONROE *is scowling*.)

HAMILTON: Thank you, sir. (*Briskly*) And so, gentlemen . . . I submit that in selling Louisiana, Napoleon broke faith with the King of Spain, and broke the law with the people of France. (*Grins at* JEFFERSON's *discomfiture and* MONROE's *baleful scowl*) And, as one attorney to another, Mr. Jefferson . . . in selling Louisiana to the United States, may not Napoleon be the purveyor of stolen goods? And Congress, if they approve of this treaty, the conveyor of stolen goods? (*Pointing to treaty*) And you, sir, in signing this treaty, the receiver of the aforementioned stolen goods?

MONROE: You put it quite harshly, sir!

HAMILTON (*seriously*): Ah, but is not the truth always harsh, Mr. Monroe?

MONROE (*angrily*): But, the real truth of the matter is we cannot afford, for our own security and advancement as a nation, to permit a powerful country like France to establish itself on our borders! Is that not so, Mr. Hamilton?

HAMILTON: My dear sir, none dare deny that, and I least of all.

JEFFERSON: Then permit me to ask of you, Mr. Hamilton . . . would you, if you were in my position, sign this treaty?

HAMILTON (*unhesitatingly*): Without the slightest hesitation, Mr. Jefferson.

JEFFERSON (*doubtfully*): And present Congress with a *fait accompli*?

HAMILTON (*nods, firmly*): Otherwise it might die a long and painful death in committee.

MONROE (*mutters*): Aye, and with the chance that, even before that, Napoleon will change his mind.

HAMILTON: Yes, I would sign this treaty (*Indicates President's chair*) . . . if I were seated in that chair. But, that would be an act of Alexander Hamilton (*With a tinge of bitterness*) . . . a man without political scruples . . . or so

I've been told . . . and not Thomas Jefferson, a man of political integrity, who would be forced to compromise some of his deepest principles by doing so. (JEFFERSON's *show of anger is engendered more by his own personal conflict than by* HAMILTON's *needling.*)

JEFFERSON (*demands*): Even so, if I did submit it to Congress unsigned, would I not still be forced to compromise with my principles?

HAMILTON (*archly*): Ah, but would you not then be diluting your guilt two million fold, by sharing it with the nation?

(JEFFERSON *looks at* HAMILTON *for a while, then slowly rises to his feet and walks away. He turns his back, looks down at the floor, struggling with himself. In silence,* HAMILTON *and* MONROE *wait for his decision;* HAMILTON *with a slight smile,* MONROE *with a dark frown. Finally,* JEFFERSON *turns to face* HAMILTON.)

JEFFERSON: And if I decide to submit the treaty to Congress without signing it beforehand, what chance would there be of their approving it? (HAMILTON *shrugs his shoulders.*) If I get your support?

HAMILTON (*with a shade of coolness*): Are you asking for that, Mr. Jefferson?

JEFFERSON (*tightly*): Yes, I'm asking for just that, Mr. Hamilton!

HAMILTON: By appealing to my patriotism, as opposed to my political interests and the interests of my party, sir?

JEFFERSON: No, sir! It would be crass stupidity on my part if I did. For never once have I ever known you to place your personal ambitions, or your party's advancement, before your country's needs.

HAMILTON (*quietly*): Thank you, Mr. Jefferson.

(JEFFERSON *walks to his chair in front of his desk and pulls out his chair. He motions* HAMILTON *to be seated behind his desk.*)

JEFFERSON: Mr. Hamilton? (*Smiles.*) I will not press you for an answer until you've studied the treaty, for it would indeed be too much to expect an attorney to ascribe to a bill of sale before examining the deed. (HAMILTON, *the copy of the treaty in his hand, walks to the desk.*) Meanwhile, if you will excuse us, Mr. Hamilton, I must pay my respects to Mrs. Monroe and welcome her back to America. (*Bows*) With your leave, sir, I shall return shortly.

(*The three exchange bows, then* JEFFERSON *and* MONROE *exit door left. When they are gone* HAMILTON *remains standing for a moment at the desk looking around the room. He sits down and leans back in the chair. With half-closed eyes, he fondles the arms of the chair. He opens his eyes, pulls the treaty closer and leans forward. His brow darkens with a frown, and a slight scowl forms on his face. When he begins to study the treaty, his face shows nothing but intense interest. This continues until there is a knock on the door right.* HAMILTON *looks up with a frown. The door opens.* LEWIS, *looking very uneasy and apologetic, closes the door behind him and walks up to the desk.*)

HAMILTON (*with a degree of irritation*): Yes, Mr. Lewis?

LEWIS: (*his voice held low, very concerned and uncertain*): I'm exceedingly sorry, Mr. Hamilton . . .

HAMILTON (*frowns*): Yes?

LEWIS: Mr. Jefferson did instruct me to see that you were not disturbed under any circumstances. But, it's Vice-President Burr, sir. He insists upon speaking with you. I did suggest, as well as I might, but . . . (*A gesture of helplessness.*)

HAMILTON (*understandingly*): I fully understand, Mr. Lewis. (*Dryly.*) After all, he is the Vice-President of the United States, isn't he?

LEWIS (*gratefully*): Yes, sir, exactly so, sir.

(HAMILTON *thinks for a moment, then, with an anticipatory smile, stands up, is about to leave the desk, but stops.*)

HAMILTON (*looks at the President's chair, amused*): Yes, Mr. Lewis, I will see Mr. Burr . . . in here.

LEWIS: Thank you, sir.

(LEWIS *exits to the reception room. When* BURR *is ushered into the office by* LEWIS, *he closes the door and goes back to the reception room.* BURR *finds* HAMILTON *very much at ease seated behind the President's desk.* BURR *takes a few steps into the room, bows with an ingratiating smile.* HAMILTON *rises to greet him.*)

BURR: Mr. Hamilton.

HAMILTON (*bows*): Mr. Burr.

BURR (*walking up to the desk*): I'm compelled to say, Mr. Hamilton, you look quite in place behind that desk.

HAMILTON: I'm glad you think so, Mr. Burr (*Motions him to a chair.*)

BURR (*as he gets seated*): In that, I'm sure, I voice the feeling of many influential people who would like nothing better than to see you there officially.

HAMILTON (*after he gets seated again*): And you, Mr. Burr, do you share their sentiments?

BURR (*feeling his way*): Did not my good friend, Mr. Pinckney, indicate that quite clearly when he met with you in New York last month?

HAMILTON: Not quite. Vaguely, I would say. But he did indicate quite clearly your intention to run for Governor of New York under the banner of the Federalist Party in the coming election. Is that what you wished to speak with me about?

BURR: That . . . among other things.

HAMILTON: Dissatisfied with the Republican Party, Mr. Burr?

BURR: Oh, it isn't a mere question of dissatisfaction, Mr. Hamilton. I must confess, I find myself more and more, as time goes by, in closer sympathy with the Federalists in matters of national policy. My party . . . or, should we say, Mr. Jefferson's party, is inclined to favor too strongly the interests of the plantation South, as opposed to the interests of the industrial North.

HAMILTON (*nods*): And that situation will continue to prevail, unless we give more power to the federal government and pay less attention to state's rights.

BURR: My sentiments entirely, sir!

HAMILTON: I'm surprised to hear that, Mr. Burr. Those are certainly not the sentiments of Mr. Jefferson, the leader of your party.

BURR: Mr. Jefferson and I disagree strongly on many issues, sir. And I firmly believe, as you do, that the wealthy class, the merchants and industrialists in the North, should be given priority and protection by the government to further their material interests, if we are ever to grow as a world power. I have refused to hide my feelings on that score, and, as a consequence, many influential members of your party, not only in New York, but in New England as a whole, have strongly urged me to join their ranks and seek the governorship of New York. But, I'm sure you are aware of that, Mr. Hamilton.

HAMILTON (smiling): Oh, yes indeed.

BURR (with a shrewd smile): Then you must also be aware that a strong gubernatorial candidate in New York on the Federalist ticket might prove to be the decisive factor in the coming presidential election. (Slowly, with marked pointedness) And, there doesn't seem to be too much doubt, in the minds of many, who will be the candidate for president under the Federalist banner.

HAMILTON (choosing to ignore the implication): Are not these the same people who wish to see the union broken up, and form a separate federation of New York and the New England States?

BURR (cautiously): There seems to be a very strong sentiment developing in that direction, Mr. Hamilton, as you must be well aware. (Shrugs his shoulders) But, who can say? It may be the only solution to the conflict of interests between the North and the South.

HAMILTON: Perhaps. But, I, for one, would prefer, if at all possible, to find another solution to the problem and keep the nation together.

BURR: Perhaps there could have been another solution, Mr. Hamilton, but it appears unlikely that the North can continue to maintain its dominance in Congress. (BURR

rises and leans over the desk to look intently at HAMILTON
as he taps the treaty with his finger.) But this . . . this will
destroy it!

HAMILTON: Oh, you know what that is, do you? (*Nods
grimly*) I must say, you come well informed.

BURR: Bah, what else but the Louisiana matter would have
brought you to the White House in the company of Mr.
Monroe? (*He leans forward.*) Mr. Hamilton, I put it to
you . . . how long can the North maintain its power over
the destinies of the nation (*Taps treaty again*) if this is
approved by Congress? How long will it be before the
Louisiana Territory—equal in area to the present size of
the nation—how long will it be before it is divided into
several, aye, perhaps a score, of states, with an over-
whelming voice in congress? I put it to you, Mr. Hamilton,
will their interests lie with the mercantile North . . . or
the agricultural South? The answer is obvious, is it not?

HAMILTON (*thoughtfully nods*): There is a great deal of
truth in what you say, Mr. Burr. I'll grant you that.

BURR (*with more boldness*): And . . . what the influential
citizens of the North dread, and justifiably so, is that the
first move of the South, with the support of the new states
in the west, will be to abolish the protective tariff and permit manufactured goods from abroad free entry into the
country.

HAMILTON (*deliberately leading him on*): Yes, it would be
to their advantage to do so, wouldn't it?

BURR: Indeed it would! And it will mean ruin and bank-
ruptcy for the North.

HAMILTON (*murmurs*): But to break up the union . . . (*He
shakes his head doubtfully.*)

BURR: Eventually it will come, Mr. Hamilton, if this treaty
is approved. In truth, I would rather see it happen now
instead of later. Should we wait for the sore to fester?
Should we wait until a bloody surgical operation remains
the only answer? No! For, mark me, sir, that day will
come. That day will surely come. (HAMILTON *looks impressed.*) Mr. Hamilton, you must see to it that *this* does

not go through. And you alone have the power to do so.

HAMILTON: Perhaps Mr. Jefferson will sign it without the approval of Congress.

BURR (*digging*): Will he?

HAMILTON (*shrugging his shoulders*): I'm sure I can't say. I am not privy to the President's council, sir.

BURR (*indicating surroundings with a sly smile*): Just reconnoitering within the enemy's lines, Mr. Hamilton?

HAMILTON (*looking at* BURR *steadily*): When I do, Mr. Burr, I carry my colors openly for all to see. (BURR'S *eyes narrow for a split second.*) Granted, that what you say may be true. But is there not a greater danger for all of us— North and South alike—to have Napoleon camped on our very doorstep?

BURR (*cautiously*): Need that be, Mr. Hamilton?

HAMILTON: How else can it be avoided, unless we possess Louisiana?

BURR: Let us suppose, Mr. Hamilton, that a separate nation, neither French, Spanish nor English . . . a friendly nation . . . is established on our borders; a nation without the power of European military behind it, one that will co-operate with the United States . . .

HAMILTON (*pursing his lips*): An interesting thought, Mr. Burr. Indeed it is. (*Doubtfully*) But Spain . . . would she tolerate that for long? Would it not jeopardize her hold on Mexico?

BURR: I have good reason to believe that Spain might even welcome it, Mr. Hamilton.

HAMILTON: Indeed?

BURR: Yes, they might even support such a move, to create a barrier state between the English in Canada on the North, and . . .

HAMILTON (*interrupts, suggestingly*): And the United States on the east, to thwart our possible expansion to the west?

BURR (*pretending the idea is new to him*): Mmm . . . I hadn't thought of it in those terms, Mr. Hamilton. But, perhaps, it might be better so, to maintain peace?

HAMILTON: Did you, by any chance, present it that way to

the Spanish ambassador, Mr. Burr?

BURR (*startled, recovers with a laugh*): Good heavens, Mr. Hamilton, what makes you think I approached the Spanish ambassador at all, on any matter?

HAMILTON: Do forgive me, Mr. Burr. Let us say it was just a presumption, thoroughly unfounded on my part, based on certain remarks you made. (*He fingers the treaty to suggest that the interview is over. BURR stands up.*) I feel very much in your debt, Mr. Burr. You have given me a great deal to think about.

BURR: I am pleased to hear that, Mr. Hamilton. May I look forward to getting your, ah, opinion, in the near future? (*HAMILTON rises slowly to his feet. His eyes narrow and his lips curl in contempt as he looks coldly at BURR.*)

HAMILTON: As for my opinion, sir . . . that need not be delayed. I am quite prepared to offer it now. My opinion sir is . . . that you are an unmitigated, black-hearted scoundrel, and it would pleasure me greatly to see you hanged as a traitor to your country!

(*BURR is completely taken aback. He is speechless for a moment, then his face tightens with rage as he looks at HAMILTON.*)

BURR (*with cold hate, slowly choosing each word*): Sir . . . I am more than ever convinced . . . there is no place in this world for both of us. And mark me . . . Mr. Hamilton . . . the time will come . . . when fate will decide which one of us stays . . . and which one of us goes. I trust that day will come soon. Good day, sir!

(*He turns and walks toward the door right. Just before he reaches the door, JEFFERSON appears in his path. BURR stops, bows stiffly to him and exits. JEFFERSON, with a puzzled look, follows his departure with his eyes. He turns to face HAMILTON with a questioning look. HAMILTON's eyes remain fastened on BURR's point of exit.*)

HAMILTON (*murmurs*): And to think that I almost . . . (*Stops*)

JEFFERSON (*coming forward*): I'm sorry you suffered an

interruption, Mr. Hamilton.

HAMILTON: By no means, Mr. Jefferson. (*He picks up treaty from desk.*) On the contrary, your esteemed Vice-President proved very helpful in assisting me to make up my mind.

JEFFERSON: About the treaty? (HAMILTON, *his eyes on the treaty, nods.*) I, too, have made up my mind.

HAMILTON (*looking up at him*): Yes?

JEFFERSON: I will not sign it before submitting it to Congress, come what may.

HAMILTON (*nods*): A wise decision, under the circumstances.

JEFFERSON: Under what circumstances, Mr. Hamilton?

(HAMILTON's *face softens as he looks at* JEFFERSON. *He appears hesitant, almost shy.*)

HAMILTON: Because (*Hesitates*) . . . Thomas . . . I have decided to use every means in my power to see this treaty approved by Congress.

(JEFFERSON *takes a long time to answer. He is touched.*)

JEFFERSON: It has been a long time . . . since you addressed me so . . . Alex. (*They regard each other sadly.*)

HAMILTON: Ah, yes. But, perhaps, we've come a long way since then . . . both of us.

C U R T A I N

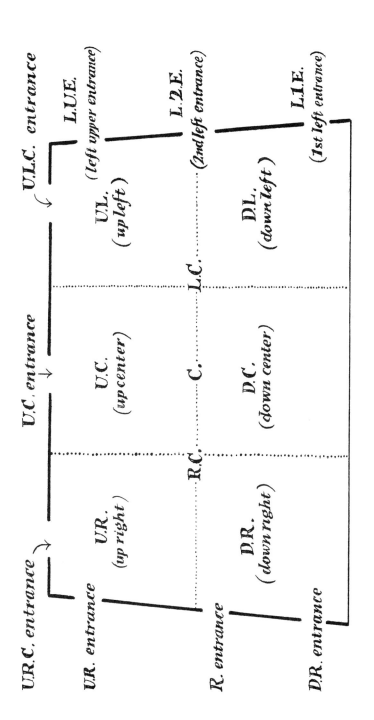

UR.C. entrance

U.C. entrance

U.L.C. entrance

UR. entrance

L.U.E. (left upper entrance)

UR. (up right)

U.C. (up center)

U.L. (up left)

R.C.

L.C.

L.2.E. (2nd left entrance)

R. entrance

D.R. (down right)

D.C. (down center)

D.L. (down left)

C.

L.1.E. (1st left entrance)

D.R. entrance

AUDIENCE

NOTES